The Process
The Refiner's Fire

KOLLIN L. TAYLOR

Copyright © 2018 Kollin L. Taylor

All rights reserved.

ISBN-13: 978-1-7908-8752-1

DEDICATION

To Christ Jesus, You are my everything.
To the prophets and prophets in training who are in the "cave" or the "wilderness", especially due to spiritual warfare, do not give up on the Lord.

CONTENTS

ACKNOWLEDGMENTS vii

PROLOGUE ix

CHAPTER 1 - ESTABLISH A FOOTHOLD 1

CHAPTER 2 - HIJACKED 7

CHAPTER 3 - TO HELL, AND BACK 26

CHAPTER 4 - UNIVERSITY OF ADVERSITY 59

CHAPTER 5 - DELIVERANCE CONFERENCE 131

CHAPTER 6 - DIVORCED 146

EPILOGUE 151

ACKNOWLEDGMENTS

Heavenly Father, thank You for the gift of life through Your Son, my Lord and Savior, Jesus the Christ. Thank You for the opportunity to share some rather painful lessons to edify Your children, and to glorify Your Son. I hated the process, but I love the product after being in the refiner's fire. I can relate to when the Holy Spirit inspired David to articulate the following profound Words:

> "Hide Thy face from my sins, and blot out all mine iniquities. Create in me a clean heart, O God; and renew a right spirit within me. **Cast me not away from Thy presence; and take not Thy Holy Spirit from me.** Restore unto me the joy of Thy salvation; and uphold me with Thy free spirit. Then will **I teach transgressors Thy ways; and sinners shall be converted unto Thee.**" ~ Psalm 51:9-13

Lord Jesus, I understand why You said to Peter, *'Simon, Simon, behold, satan hath desired to have you, that he may sift you as wheat: But I have prayed for thee, that thy faith fail not: and when thou art converted, strengthen thy brethren.'* ~ Luke 22:31-32 Thank You for Your prayers, and for this opportunity to strengthen my brothers and sisters, we need it and You.

It is often said that a teacher is silent during a test. Thank You Lord for not removing Your Holy Spirit from me and for never totally remaining silent. If it were not for You, the enemy's relentless onslaught would have destroyed me. Thank You for Your faithfulness in seeing me through the worst season of my life. Jesus, I look forward to the day when every knee bows, and every tongue publicly confesses that You are Lord.

Thanks to everyone who helped me during this tribulation, especially with your prayers. Special thanks to Charlotte; you have a way of usually being the better friend in most and possibly all of your friendships, which include ours. Thanks also to Adele, Santa, Sam, Linda, and Carah. Nadine, you are a blessing beyond measure.

All Bible quotes are from the King James Version. **Bold** and ALL CAPITALIZED texts are for added emphasis.

The Process: The Refiner's Fire is the follow-up to:

Raised in the Wilderness: Rogue Reformers, Rallying the Remnant

So, You Want to be a Prophet... ARE YOU CRAZY?

PROLOGUE

"For we wrestle not against flesh and blood, but against principalities, against powers, against the rulers of the darkness of this world, against spiritual wickedness in high places." ~ Ephesians 6:13

I loved and watched numerous martial arts films during my life; I even practiced martial arts. Yet, despite that (former) love, I never loved fighting. I hated bullying and injustice, and I still do. I wanted to study martial arts as a child but that was not possible where I grew up in Jamaica. Things changed after I joined the United States Army and started practicing Karate at my first duty station. I wanted to work hard to accelerate the advancement process. Sadly, to my chagrin, my efforts and dedication resulted in me taking my first test for promotion six months later, just like everyone else. I would not consider myself as being impatient, but I also liked track and field, most of all the 100m dash, where the objective is to finish the race as fast as possible. I prefer to work twice as hard if it will get me to a goal at least twice as fast. Consequently, that type of mindset made this spiritual marathon battle even more arduous and frustrating at times. I eventually felt like the Lord had a set time for me to endure this trial, and no amount of effort was going to cause Him to deliver me a day sooner than He had earmarked. In addition, I preferred to fight on my feet, but I was being made to wrestle with my back on the ground.

It is said that most fights end up on the ground. My mindset was to put someone on the ground by knocking him out. I liked boxing but I never liked when a fight needed the judges' opinions, the same thing goes for Mixed Martial Arts (MMA). I had very little sympathy for fighters who claimed the judges robbed them of a decision, even when that was the case. Fighters should secure victory before the final bell rings.

When I watched MMA, I appreciated the skills of the grapplers and submission fighters. But I favored those who specialized in the standup arts. Just like Ephesians 6:12 states, I was in the toughest battle of my life against an enemy who liked to wrestle. I had done a lot of sparring in martial arts, but I also spent half of my life (as of the date of this writing) in the United States Army. During that time I spent a lot of time fighting simulated battles that included simulators, pyrotechnics, and blank ammunition. We also conducted Live Fire Exercises (LFX) that were carefully planned to include safety measures to prevent fratricide. After all, the goal was never to shoot each other. I spent six years in combat zones where people tried to kill me. Yet, with the hundreds of rocket, mortar, small arms fire, and Improvised Explosive Device attacks I went through, I slept better than the hell I am about to describe. One of the worst things was this battle was against an invisible enemy who never slept. I endured sleep deprivation in the Army, but nothing compares to this.

When a "ground fighter" faces a "standup fighter", a part of the ground fighter's strategy is to take the fight to the ground, even if it means absorbing a few blows to do so. A Jujitsu practitioner may intentionally use a technique called "pulling guard" to bring an opponent to the ground. Likewise, the devil wanted to wrestle me to the ground and keep me there because he wanted to prevent me from advancing in life. The saying "Tap, snap, or nap" is a part of MMA. If refers to ending a fight by causing the opponent to quit by tapping out, breaking a body part to cause the opponent to quit or the referee to stop the fight, or, knocking the opponent out with either punches or a variety of chokeholds. The enemy was determined to fight dirty, pull me down to his stronghold, and use any means necessary to cause me to walk away from the ministry. Most of all, the enemy wanted me to walk away from the Lord; on the grounds that He had failed to protect and deliver me from the evil I was enduring.

Prior to Job's tribulation, it was the Lord who recommended putting Job to the test, within certain limits. During Job's testing his wife told him to curse God, and die (Job 2:9). That recommendation seemingly reveals why the devil never directly afflicted Job's wife. I knew the enemy was trying to push me to the point of cursing God, but I did not curse God. I confess there were times when I openly expressed my frustration and anger because I knew He could end the torments but was allowing them to continue. I heard the testimony of Michael Chriswell, who shared a recording of him crying out to the Lord, asking "Why?" during his tribulation. Most of his torments came through people, but he also dealt with devils. This testimony is a combination of Michael's and another minister named Kevin L.A. Ewing. In Kevin's case, he wrestled with a witch and devils. Kevin testified of being so tormented in his bedroom that he slept on his sofa with the lights on. I can relate to both men's testimonies, very well. I have endured thousands of witchcraft and demonic attacks, some of which I will present as you join me on this journey.

I was an in-your-face stand up fighter going against an invisible enemy, one who liked to wrestle with me while I slept. The devil did everything possible inside of the parameters the Lord established to put me to the test. Jesus said the thief comes to steal, kill, and destroy (John 10:10). I would be dead if the Lord had allowed the enemy to kill me, especially because I was so stubborn. In fact, there was a time when the enemy brought me close to death.

On this occasion, I was sleeping on my (home) office floor when I experienced what some people call "sleep paralysis". However, this was a demonic attack because I woke up with a devil's hand around my neck, squeezing so tightly that it felt like my eyes were bulging to the point of exploding. I could not move or speak so I spiritually called upon the Lord by thinking of His name by (mentally) saying, "Jesus, Jesus, Jesus, Je…" Sadly, the Lord did not immediately come to my rescue like during previous attacks. I began to see the heavens opening up, and I felt at peace because I knew I was going to be with the Lord. I realized the enemy was trying to induce fear, but on the contrary, the enemy saw my faith and confidence in my salvation. It was like when Jesus was on the cross, sacrificing Himself for us, and He proclaimed, *'Father, into Thy hands I commend My Spirit.'* ~ Luke 23:46. I was lying on the floor, with my back pressed to the ground by a devil that was squeezing the life out of me. Unlike times past when the Lord intervened, this time He was simply ensuring the devil did not kill me. The devil relented upon realizing I did not fear him, but was willing to die because of my faith in Christ Jesus.

The enemy likes to "wrestle" (Ephesians 6:12-13). As a countermeasure, we are instructed to put on the whole armor of God. So, while the enemy wants to pull us down into a dirty fight, we are directed to stand on principles such as our salvation, righteousness, and the truth. On another note, some ministers will tell you to put on the full armor of God daily (Ephesians 6:10-20). I wore modern body armor when I was in the military. I only had to put armor on because I had taken it off. Therefore, I keep my spiritual armor on at all times. Also, our weapons' arming status would change depending on whether we were on or off our military base. We had to "lock and load", with our weapons on safe, when going off base. On the contrary, our weapons remained on safe when we were on the base, but no rounds were chambered and we removed the magazine from the weapon's magazine well. When it comes to spiritual warfare, our armor is never removed and our spiritual weapons always remain locked and loaded. That reminds me of when Paul wrote: "Preach the Word; be instant in season, out of season; reprove, rebuke, exhort with all long suffering and doctrine." ~ 2 Timothy 4:2

"The Process: The Refiner's Fire" exposes some of the abominable things people, including professing Christians and even ministers, do. It is a summary of events I endured from 2015 to 2018, with most of the emphasis on 2018, the year I launched the major counteroffensive. The enemy counts on our ignorance of his devices, but, once uncovered, he oftentimes launches vicious counterattacks. For two decades the military trained me to wage carnal warfare from the tactical to the strategic level, but I was going to experience a battle in a totally different realm. It was reminiscent of the 1987 film, "Predator", where some highly trained men found themselves in a South American jungle, fighting an enemy from out of this world. The enemy initially left them feeling outgunned and outclassed, until they discovered it bled, which meant it could die… While devils are immortal, they can suffer, which is why I love one of the many Scripture the devil hates, Revelation 20:10.

THE PROCESS: THE REFINER'S FIRE

Most of the books I was inspired to write were completed within a week, some in as little as two days. Three notable exceptions are "Australia: My Journey Down Under", which covers the two-week span I spent in Australia in 2013, "Survival", took a month, and the narrative, "The Anatomy of a Heartbreak: When SAMson met Delilah", six months. "The Process: The Refiner's Fire" is in a class by itself. I have had many concepts for books, some of which remain as unpublished manuscripts. I had a concept for writing a book with samples of demonic dreams and visions and their interpretations. But in September 2018, the Lord inspired me to share more, a whole lot more than I ever thought I would publicly share. In all the published books to date, I have never experienced writer's block or lack of motivation in a project. I was dragging my feet on this project because I was waiting for the victory the Lord had promised me before starting it. However, the Lord had Charlotte tell me to watch an interview, one I had seen in 2013. The Lord used the interview to guide me to write about my tribulation while I was still in it. Such a move epitomizes that "…without faith it is impossible to please Him: for he that cometh to God must believe that He is, and that He is a rewarder of them that diligently seek Him." ~ Hebrews 11:6. "The Process: The Refiner's Fire" is about seeking the Lord during a tribulation. I had written seven pages when the Lord also sent Carah. After that encounter, 7 pages turned to 27 pages within 24 hours, and 47 pages within 48 hours. Then, like the last two books, the Lord gave me the manuscript's final page count; 140 pages are the most of any of my published books to date. I had a title in mind, until the Lord weighed in and gave me the title, His chosen title, yesterday. It reminds me of when the Lord said to Abraham, *'Get thee out of thy country, and from thy kindred, and from thy father's house, unto a land that I will shew thee.'* ~ Genesis 12:1. I was not sure where I was going, I only knew I needed to go and the Lord would be with me.

Today is October 19, 2018 and I am still going through intense spiritual warfare. Yet, the Lord has brought me through some horrible and seemingly unspeakable experiences, things that will stretch anyone's faith in the Lord. In a lot of ways, this is the follow-up to the recently published "So, You Want to be a Prophet… ARE YOU CRAZY?" If you are familiar with Social Aloe Ministries, you will know the tagline is, "Glorifying God. Exposing the devil." "The Process: The Refiner's Fire" is about to do both. Many people try to shame the devil. I mostly want to use this book to expose his oftentimes covert plans and operations, which are meant to ruin your life. Some of these situations may seem bleak to the point of hopelessness, but the devil is no match for Jesus, the Christ, our Savior, Redeemer, and Lord.

CHAPTER 1

ESTABLISH A FOOTHOLD

"Neither give place to the devil." ~ Ephesians 4:26

I wondered how and even when this story will end, yet not initially sure where to begin. When I was inspired to write "The Anatomy of a Heartbreak: When SAMson met Delilah", I was not sure why the impacts of the events were so severe. I have healed from that situation, but it plays an important role in what I am going through. The book's title says "…SAMson…" to highlight "SAM", which is a pseudonym. This may come as a surprise. I stated in the book that SAM was also an acronym, but I had no idea what it meant at the time. The Lord finally revealed three years later that SAM stood for Social Aloe Ministries. I was clueless at the time that the Lord was going to call me to serve Him, within a few months. I finished the book in 2012, having been humbled, but still a lukewarm Christian. I never wanted to experience heartbreak again. I literally got down on my knees and asked the Lord for a wife of His choosing. I also asked Him for a house and a car. The Lord has fulfilled the latter two requests in accordance with the desires of my heart.

As evidenced in "The Anatomy of a Heartbreak: When SAMson met Delilah", I started having more prophetic dreams and visions, but I was ignorant of 1 John 4:1. I learned the hard way why it was important to know that Scripture. When I asked the Lord for a wife, I had a vision of a young lady's face. Then, lo and behold, she contacted me about a week later. Based on recent supernatural experiences, it seemed as if she was the answer to my prayers. We started communicating with increased frequency and intensity in a long distance relationship. She seemed like an incredible woman, but I had a few concerns. Then, one day after recently returning from Jamaica, I was in Miami Beach, standing on the 10th floor balcony of a hotel, looking at the Atlantic Ocean. I suddenly heard a voice telling me to jump and I would land on my feet like a cat. It seemed very plausible, but I knew I would go splat if I had obeyed the voice. Arguably, it was the first time I had heard a supernatural voice, like that. Then I heard another voice, similar, yet different, say, "Put a parachute around your heart." I did not immediately understand its meaning, but I found out within 24 hours. I was watching a show where a woman was going to break up with a man she said was smothering her. Sadly, the man was trying to love her but she needed to heal from previous relationships. Even though it was a long distance relationship, I felt as if the young lady thought I was smothering her. I brought it up the next time we communicated and she said she felt smothered. I wondered how in the world I could have smothered her with such great distance and limited contact. I realized then that the second voice I heard on the balcony was the Lord's. At that moment I lived the reality of my heart, seemingly made of glass, being dropped from the 10th floor balcony, without a parachute, and shattering into innumerable pieces on the pavement.

Shortly afterwards, several supernatural occurrences indicated a war between two kingdoms. I was walking one night, nursing a second heartbreak, which was more devastating than the first, when I heard a voice say, "If God loved you, He would not allow you to suffer so much." I did not come into agreement with the spirit because I knew it was demonic. It was indicative of a war over my gifts and calling, even though they were still mysteries to me at the time. It is worthy to note I was led to believe I would get reunited with the young lady who had suddenly, and unceremoniously, dumped me, the second major heartbreak in less than a year. Within a few months, in the beginning of 2013, I had my "burning bush moment" when the Lord called me to serve Him. Briefly stated, I was walking by a chapel one night in Kuwait when I heard a voice say, "Minister to the people." I stopped, looked around in the dark, to see who had spoken to me. I saw no one. I managed to take about two to three more steps when I again heard, "Minister to the people." I realized it was the Lord, but based on my history, I thought He had made a mistake by selecting me. I resumed walking, shaking my head in disbelief, but after taking about two to three more steps, I heard His voice again. Without changing His Words, the Lord said, "Minister to the people." I accepted His calling without asking for or receiving any additional instructions. Saying yes to the Lord meant I instantly and officially became an enemy to the kingdom of darkness.

I had recently begun journaling based on a friend's recommendation to cope with the first heartbreak. The journal became the manuscript for "The Anatomy of a Heartbreak: When SAMson met Delilah". Journaling remains a staple of my relationship with the Lord (see Habakkuk 2:2-3). I strongly recommend prophets, or anyone with the gift of prophecy, write down their encounters with and revelations from the Lord, unless the Lord forbids it (see Revelation 10:4). A journal also helps to decipher and recognize how the Lord may encode His dreams and visions to you, unless He does not communicate to you in the form of parables (see Numbers 12:6-8). For example, the Lord could have simply told me the young lady was going to break my heart. Instead, He told me to put a parachute around my heart. There was a time when I felt like the Lord communicated to me through dreams more than visions. But that was because I was more diligent about recording the details of my dreams. Increased enemy activity stemming from visions has caused me to notice visions I would not have previously discerned or may have simply ignored.

There are basically two types of visions: with eyes opened or closed. In a vision with the eyes open, it is like a photograph or video clip, much like a hologram where you can see the translucent supernatural image that is superimposed on the natural world. A vision with eyes closed can occur while awake, such as while praying, or asleep. Hence, what some people think was a dream was actually a vision. Having a vision while sleeping explains why sometimes the Bible uses the term "vision of the night". You may recall Elihu rebuking Job for justifying himself instead of God, by saying, *'For God speaketh once, yea twice, yet man perceiveth it not. In a dream, IN A VISION OF THE NIGHT, when deep sleep falleth upon men, in slumberings upon the bed; Then He openeth the ears of men, and sealeth their instruction, That He may withdraw man from his purpose, and hide pride from man.'* ~ Job 33:14-17

Journaling has significantly helped me fulfill my calling from the Lord. The following serves as an example of the importance for why Christians, especially ministers, should keep a journal: "Now the rest of the acts of Solomon, first and last, are they not written in the book of Nathan the prophet, and in the prophecy of Ahijah the Shilonite, and in the visions of Iddo the seer against Jeroboam the son of Nebat?" ~ 2 Chronicles 9:29. We know more about Solomon because those prophets wrote about him in their journals. This book would be much thicker if I were to share every dream and vision from the last year. Instead, I will rely on the Holy Spirit to order my steps and bring to my recollection experiences that He wants me to share either briefly or entirely. But my journal is ready if the Holy Spirit directs me to consult it.

I used to wonder how to discern the differences between a dream or vision from the devil, my soul, or the Lord. Most of what I have seen from others regarding interpreting dreams and visions are geared towards things from the Lord. Well, after enduring thousands of demonic attacks, the following will help you to discern the differences:

- A dream in black and white is indicative of an enemy plot, which, like all enemy plans, you should immediately pray against upon waking.
- Nudity, with exposed sexual organs, and, dreams that involve sexual activity.
- Eating, especially if you were forced to eat, or, if the food involves eating raw meat or food that would not survive a food inspection. The same applies to drinking. Both are linked to when Paul wrote, "Ye cannot drink the cup of the Lord, and the cup of devils: ye cannot be partakers of the Lord's table, and of the table of devils." ~ 1 Corinthians 10:21
- Communicating with deceased people, which is a form of the forbidden practice of necromancy.
- Doing things in dreams you would not do in your waking moments, especially if you do not desire to do those things. Yet, "you" do them in encounters, sometimes against your will, as if you cannot stop it or say no. You become an unwilling participant.

- People do not look or act like themselves. This is because evil spirits are masquerading as these individuals to gain your trust. In some cases, you have a sense for who the people are, even though you cannot see their faces. Such dreams or visions are indicative of witchcraft activities meant to pollute your life or destiny by people trying to mask their identity.
- Encounters under the cover of low light or darkness, oftentimes coupled with a feeling of fear. But God has not given us a spirit of fear (2 Timothy 1:7). The Lord can reveal terrible things but give us the grace to endure them without fear. Like David appropriately said, "Yea, though I walk through the valley of the shadow of death, I will fear no evil: for Thou art with me; Thy rod and Thy staff they comfort me." ~ Psalm 23:4
- An overwhelming feeling of hopelessness, which may come from being in a place where you (seemingly) cannot escape. You may even call upon the name of the Lord to no avail, as if you are in a place that is out of His reach and jurisdiction. Lies are obviously of the devil.
- Closed or blocked doors, being in a vehicle that runs out of fuel or the tires go flat, being held back by an invisible force or being bound or binding yourself.
- Swimming, being tossed to and fro in water, getting pulled under water even to the point of being on the verge of drowning or getting overcome by a crushing tidal wave. You may also find yourself being in the rain or standing in bodies of water in unusual places.
- Realizing that everyone in the room or environment, even if you do not know them are acting strange. Again, devils masquerading as people.
- Incoherent encounters that result in confusion and a lack of peace. Most of the things seem inconsequential, then something suddenly happens Remember, "For God is not the author of confusion, but of peace, as in all churches of the saints." ~ 1 Corinthians 14:33

The devil tries to corrupt and/or counterfeit the things of God. For instance, when the Lord has forged covenants with people, or given them blessings, while they were asleep. The Lord put Adam to sleep, removed one of his ribs, woke him up, and blessed him with Eve, whom He created from that rib (Genesis 2). The Lord also put Abraham to sleep when forging a covenant with him (Genesis 15). The enemy tries to steal things from us while we sleep. If we do not rebuke him in the spiritual encounter, or upon waking, he will bring curses upon our life. Sadly, many Christians are not progressing as they should because the enemy is covertly robbing them while they sleep. I had an appalling dream the same night the previously book, "So, You Want to be a Prophet… ARE YOU CRAZY?" was published. I saw my iPad in a darkened room with my email application open. I reached for the screen to open a message, but the message suddenly disappeared, as if someone hacked into my email and deleted the message. I woke up knowing the enemy was attacking the book to prevent people from reading it. Many people have had similar experiences but have not realized those unchallenged spiritual attacks produced adversities in real life. I know what the enemy did to me so I take pleasure in warning others, so they will not to suffer needlessly, and to ruin the devil's life.

The aforementioned scenarios regarding how the enemy might attack are from the chronicles of my personal experiences. It is purely by God's grace and mercy why I am still alive, and of a sound mind and body articulating these things to you. On another note, the Lord made it clear that the young lady I saw in a vision when I asked Him for a wife was not the woman He had ordained as my wife. I started this saga by mentioning her because, even without her knowledge or involvement, the devil used her as a major weapon against me. You will see why and how, soon. Please join me as I present some things that many people, to include professing Christians who believe in a supernatural God, will not believe. I will also answer the frequently debated question regarding if a Christian can have a demon. Yet, arguably, the question is truly if a demon can have a Christian because a believer is free to choose.

CHAPTER 2

HIJACKED

*"Lest satan should get an advantage of us:
for we are not ignorant of his devices." ~ 2 Corinthians 2:11*

The devil has done some very dumb things, such as trying to unseat the true and living God from His throne, but he is still a strategic tactician. Thankfully, his wisdom is foolishness in comparison to the Lord's wisdom. One such example is how the Lord thwarted the devil's plans with the young lady he brought into my life, packaged like a gift from God. She was meant to cause serious negative long-term impacts on my life. The third chapter of "So, You Want to be a Prophet… ARE YOU CRAZY?" tells of the incident with another young lady in a church. She was the one the Lord highlighted to me and said, "She is My daughter." I only partially knew the magnitude of the revelation. It was not the first time I had seen her, but it was the first time the Lord had revealed anything about her to me. Things would have been different if the Lord had revealed that to me the first time I saw His daughter. During our initial encounter, I was faithfully waiting on the other young lady and was basically blind to any other woman. The Lord could have pointed out His daughter as being the woman He had chosen to be my wife and there would have been issues because I was already hooked on satan's counterfeit. A part of the devil's strategy is to block our blessings, by any means necessary.

Some people find certain things unbelievable because they are not clearly stated in the Bible. For example, while Matthew 3:16-17 and 1 John 5:7 give clear examples of the Holy Trinity, the term "Holy Trinity" is not in the Bible. I had a conversation with the first young lady regarding abstinence, which she said was easy for her. However, she had periodic dreams of a sexual nature. I was ignorant that meant I was seeing someone's wife... By the way, I am not uncovering the young lady. On the contrary, I am uncovering the devil and how he operates. I will also uncover myself in the process, more so than her. Evil thrives in the dark and I am letting the Light shine on everything. Also, like the Lord said, *'My people are destroyed for lack of knowledge...'* ~ Hosea 4:6.

During my first year of high school in Jamaica, the sexual education teacher told us about puberty, masturbation, and nocturnal emissions (also known as "wet dreams"). She made it seemed so natural, like a rite of passage. I had never heard of such thing and desired to have a "wet dream", which seemed like a gift at the time. However, I want to warn you about the dangers of masturbation and wet dreams. This is because there was a dangerous and life-altering tree in the Garden of Eden called "the tree of the knowledge of good and evil". The sexual education class is comparable to a fruit salad from that very tree. The sexual education teacher showed us a drawing of a man masturbating. My best friend at the time told me he had done it and how to do it. I will not pretend that I was innocent because I had been exposed to sex and sexual material prior to the class. Wretchedly, I was exposed to hidden sexual knowledge I was better off without. This started years, and I mean decades, of me engaging in masturbation, even when I did not have to. Tragically, I only found out about the evils of masturbation and wet dreams in the last two years. Both represent, at a minimum, possibly forging a covenant with the devil. At the other extreme, both acts are used to forge and reinstate covenants with him. Many Christians are saved, but their minds and genitals are not because they keep engaging in demonically motivated sexual behavior. Each sinful act is indicative of putting one's body on an altar to the devil. The enemy uses these things to cause us to sin by violating the following, and therefore giving himself access to us, or at least parts of us:

> "Know ye not that your bodies are the members of Christ? Shall I then take the members of Christ, and make them the members of

an harlot? God forbid. What? Know ye not that he which is joined to an harlot is one body? *'For two'*, saith He, *'shall be one flesh.'* But he that is joined unto the Lord is one spirit. **Flee fornication.** Every sin that a man doeth is without the body; but he that committeth fornication sinneth against his own body.

What? Know ye not that your body is the temple of the Holy Ghost which is in you, which ye have of God, and **ye are not your own**? For ye are bought with a price: therefore glorify God in your body, and in your spirit, which are God's." ~ 1 Corinthians 6:15-20

"I beseech you therefore, brethren, by the mercies of God, that ye present your bodies a living sacrifice, holy, acceptable unto God, which is your reasonable service." ~ Romans 12:1

Many people disagree, but **based on personal experiences, no one can convince me that a Christian cannot have a devil or devils.** I was deceived into thinking masturbation was not a sin. I felt like as long as I was not having sex with another person, I was not sinning against the Lord. Well, one of the fallacies with such belief is that masturbation requires a source of lust. I have publicly professed to having violated all ten of the Lord's Commandments. I have never seen someone violate one Commandment without simultaneously violating at least one other. There were times when engaging in masturbation elevated my sin from fornication to adultery. So, in many ways, like a lot of other people who say they have never done it, I was an adulterer. Another way many people, to include myself, have committed adultery is based on when Jesus said, *'But I say unto you, that whosoever looketh on a woman to lust after her hath committed adultery with her already in his heart.'* ~ Matthew 5:28. I also need to warn about a common trend of dating someone whose divorce is not finalized. Simple stated, it is a form of adultery and those involved in these types of situations will face righteous judgment. The Lord also commanded us to not commit murder (Exodus 20:13). You may feel great because you have never killed anyone. However, "Whosoever hateth his brother is a murderer: and ye know that no murderer hath eternal life abiding in him." ~ 1 John 3:15. Also, Jesus said, *'Ye have heard that it was said of them of old time, 'Thou shalt not kill; and whosoever shall kill shall be in danger of the judgment': But I say unto you, 'That* *whosoever is angry with his brother without a cause shall be in danger of the judgment: and whosoever shall say to his brother, 'Raca', shall be in danger of the council: but whosoever shall say, 'Thou fool', shall be in danger of hell fire. Therefore if thou bring thy gift to the altar, and there rememberest that thy brother hath ought against thee; Leave there thy gift before the altar, and go thy way; first be reconciled to thy brother, and then come and offer thy gift.'* ~ Matthew 5:21-24

The above illustrates that in our unique ways, we all need a Savior in Christ Jesus. Do not make the prideful mistake of telling someone not to judge you for being in a relationship with someone else's spouse. There is a difference between having sinned and living in sin. Do not harden our heart against the conviction of your sins. Two of the functions of the Holy Spirit are to convict us of our sins, and of our righteousness (John 16:7-10). Our righteousness without the Lord is as filthy rags to the Father (Isaiah 64:6).

In another vein, condemnation is from the devil, which is one reason why I am sharing these intimate details of my life. There is also power in the redemptive qualities of Jesus' blood. Many Christians are in bondage to the devil because of "secret sins". We all can admit that it is really tragic when sin ensnares a minister, but because of pride, the minister continues living in unrepentant sin until his or her death. While it is not necessary to confess our sins to others in great detail, every Christian should know how Jesus feels about hypocrisy. Contrary to popular belief, the Lord's main issue with the Pharisees was not because they were religious. The Lord clearly told people to do as the Pharisees instructed, but they should not do what the Pharisees did because therein lied their hypocrisy (Matthew 23). They looked holy but were unclean, like tombs filled with dead men's bones. Jesus later warned that hypocrisy was the leaven of the Pharisees (Luke 12:1). It is hypocritical for a minister to confess his or her sins to the Lord in private, but publicly act as if he or she did not need the Lord's forgiveness. Again, many Christians are in bondage to the devil because of secrets. Never forget the following:

> "Now the Lord is that Spirit: and where the Spirit of the Lord is, there is liberty." ~ 2 Corinthians 3:17

> "There is therefore now no condemnation to them which are in Christ Jesus, who walk not after the flesh, but after the Spirit." ~ Romans 8:1

THE PROCESS: THE REFINER'S FIRE

A part of my reluctance to answer the Lord's call was I was uncertain of who was calling. I also thought He had made a mistake based on my sinful past. Undoubtedly, these words were eventually fulfilled in my own changed life: "Therefore if any man be in Christ, he is a new creature: old things are passed away; behold, all things are become new." ~ 2 Corinthians 5:17. When anyone is in the presence of the holy God, pure and perfect in all His ways, they get to understand these reactions:

> "When Simon Peter saw it, he fell down at Jesus' knees, saying, *'Depart from me; for I am a sinful man, O Lord.'*" ~ Luke 5:8

> "Then said I, *'Woe is me! For I am undone; because I am a man of unclean lips, and I dwell in the midst of a people of unclean lips: for mine eyes have seen the King, the Lord of hosts.'*" ~ Isaiah 6:5

Many people say a devil cannot dwell in a Christian because the Holy Spirit dwells in the Christian, and He, the Holy Spirit, will not dwell in an unclean vessel. I will make some brief comments on the subject instead of a protracted discussion. If some professing Christians are not being demonically influenced or oppressed, what is the reason for their demonic behavior? Arguably, if the Holy Spirit does not dwell in unclean places, He would have never entered into us. When the Holy Spirit enters an unclean vessel, it will not remain unclean, but sanctification is oftentimes a process. When the woman with the issue of blood touched the hem of Jesus' clothes, by Law, she should have polluted Him. However, He cleansed her instead. Likewise, through the sanctification process, the Holy Spirit will cleanse the vessel He dwells in. It is reminiscent of Christ entering the temple and seeing the filthiness. He took some time to make a scourge, and then He systematically cleansed His Father's house and restored it to a house of prayer.

I also had a radical experience like the woman with the issue of blood, but without even seeking the Lord about it. After faithfully masturbating for decades, I was in bed one morning in 2014 when I suddenly sneezed. I distinctly felt something pass through my right nostril. Whatever I felt, it was not a physical substance. I soon realized I had completely lost the desire to masturbate. Some people will have an issue with me calling an unclean spirit a name based on its characteristics. But, the Lord radically delivered me from a "spirit of masturbation", something that had been driving me to masturbate for decades. For the scoffers, when Jesus delivered the woman who had been bound for 18 years, He called the unclean spirit a *'spirit of infirmity'* (Luke 13:11). In addition, other named unclean spirits, based on their character traits, include, a "spirit of jealousy" (Numbers 5:14), a "spirit of fear" (2 Timothy 1:7), etc. You can try to dispute this report, but I will not join you because the Lord delivered me, and, I do not debate the Word of God.

The Word of God establishes my beliefs instead of my beliefs establishing the Word of God. The devil is a strategic thinker, and he had a few more things up his sleeve to try to keep me in bondage to him. Therefore, while getting delivered from a "spirit of masturbation" was great news, the deliverance process was not complete. There was an unknown demonic behemoth lurking beneath the surface. Many people believe the devil cannot make people do anything against their will. I am about to make the devil mad by exposing that too. I would not sin so the devil came up with ways to bring sin to me, in part because of my ignorance at the time about the his subtle yet sinister devices.

As previously stated, the young lady I was initially interested in had dreams of a sexual nature. Some people cannot relate to such matters. It either does not happen to them, or, they may have had dreams where someone (a spirit) initiated sex with them but they rejected it. A part of me holding on to the young lady was based on an experience I had on January 23, 2014, at around 4:30 a.m. It was great that the Lord took me back through my journal to reveal things. That was a part of why the devil tried destroying my journal on several occasions. This is one of the devil's eschatological strategies. It is comparable to **the devil over decades trying to ban and destroy every copy of the Bible, a strategy he will continue employing until his end. For example while having an electronic Bible is convenient, it is easier to modify its contents, and at any opportune time, pull the plug on (electronic) Bibles.** Therefore, I recommend having a printed version of the Bible. But there are several reasons why I know that while the enemy's plans will have a significant impact, they will ultimately fail because:

- *'This is the covenant that I will make with them after those days'*, saith the Lord, *'I will put My Laws into their hearts, and in their minds will I write them.'* ~ Hebrews 10:16
- *'But the Comforter, which is the Holy Ghost, Whom the Father will send in My name, He shall teach you all things, and bring all things to your remembrance, whatsoever I have said unto you.'* ~ Jesus (John 14:26)
- *'Howbeit when He, the Spirit of truth, is come, He will guide you into all truth: for He shall not speak of Himself; but whatsoever He shall hear, that shall He speak: and He will shew you things to come. He shall glorify Me: for He shall receive of Mine, and shall shew it unto you. All things that the Father hath are Mine: therefore said I, that He shall take of Mine, and shall shew it unto you.'* ~ Jesus (John 16:13-15)
- *'Heaven and earth shall pass away, but My Words shall not pass away.'* ~ Jesus (Matthew 24:35)

So, on January 23, 2014, I woke up feeling as if the Lord had placed something in me. It was like God had established a spiritual connection between the young lady and me. It was like she was in me and I was in her, as if we had become one, in a sort of spiritual marriage. The experience reminds me of when Jesus said, *'Abide in Me, and I in you...'* ~ John 15:4. It was the closest I had ever felt to her. However, years later, the Lord revealed to me that the experience was of the devil. **We like to blame the devil when we receive things that we do not want or like, but thank the Lord for the desires of our heart, typically without testing the spirit.** Shortly after that seemingly wonderful occurrence, I was shocked when this dream resulted in nocturnal emission. It was perplexing that a man of my age had such a dream. In addition, I was not battling lust and sexual urges. I thought it was simply a natural physical reaction to finally being totally celibate, which included abstaining from masturbation.

Oddly, a month later, it happened again. Even more perplexing was that it kept happening every month at around the same time, always on time like a woman's menstrual cycle. Interestingly, I did not feel a buildup of sexual desires at around the time of these dreams. I also noticed that the dreams usually involved a woman from my past. Consequently, the dreams seemed more like a flashback instead of a real time event, which also contributed to me not resisting these dreams. I liken the dreams to a menstrual cycle. However, it is not because there was a buildup in my body like a menstrual cycle that needed release. A menstrual cycle is oftentimes described as a "visitor". Little did I know at the time that the monthly visitations were a satanic bill collector, coming by my house to collect its monthly payment. It was also like receiving a monthly bill in an envelope laced with ricin. In addition to stealing my virtues, the enemy was trying to get me sexually aroused so that I would resume sinning by masturbating. However, when the Lord cast the spirit of masturbation out, the desire to masturbate left also. The enemy was trying to get me to sin to let that sin back into my life, which would have made things worse for me.

Sadly, while masturbation was out, permanently, I was unaware of the other monster that would lurk, undetected, for two more years. Before I continue, let me share a warning I was inspired to post about masturbation:

> There are times when I publicly share things with others that you, my viewing audience, never get to experience. The following was almost filed away in that category. I recently saw someone who had posted a video on YouTube about relationships. The video was about if masturbation is a sin. I did not watch the video when I first became aware of it, but I felt as if I did, I would have a lot to say on the matter. The Lord revealed to me a few months ago that He had called me to set the captives free. And, as it is written, "…Through knowledge shall the just be delivered." ~ Proverbs 11:9(KJV) I was not led to discuss, at least not directly, whether masturbation is a sin. However, based on the following commentary I posted, you may no longer want to debate if masturbation is a sin:

> "Masturbation is one of the many sneaky tools the devil uses to slowly ruin people's lives. It is also one of the many potential reasons why some people cannot sustain relationships, get married, or have a peaceful marriage.

> While this does not apply to everyone, some people who are struggling with masturbation are dealing with what is called a "spiritual husband or wife". It is an impure spirit that acts like a person's spouse and drives others away from that individual. It is like a protective spouse, but more accurately like a predator guarding its prey. That is one of the reasons why some people are

dealing with negative voices telling them that for example; no will love them, they won't get married and they are unattractive. All such things are designed to put a person in bondage to masturbation.

The impure spirit ("spirit spouse") is one of the underlying spiritual reasons why someone may have had great relationships, there was talk of marriage, and then the other person suddenly ended the relationship, without warning. These incidences may deteriorate a person's self-esteem, and may result in them turning to masturbation as a viable option. This can also be compared to some people attempting to drown their sorrows with alcohol or in a pint of ice cream. The person who left may have claimed he or she was not ready to settle down, but six months later married someone else. Others will look back at why they ended the relationship, and to their surprise, realize the reason does not stand the test of time. Yet, some will testify of coming under spiritual attacks in the (former) relationship, even if they may not articulate it as such. An example is suddenly feeling resentment towards someone he or she adored.

One of the ways to tell of the severity of the issue is to stop masturbating, which may be difficult, and see what happens. If you start having sexually explicit dreams, it indicates a serious spiritual attack from the enemy. Sex of any kind, to include self-pleasure or in a dream represents a covenant, either with the Lord or the devil. A sexual dream may seem innocuous, but it is also an attack of the enemy, even when a married person has a dream about his or her spouse. Some people experience what is referred to as "sleep paralysis", which is actually a demonic attack. For many people, some of whom will not admit it, these attacks are sexual in nature, from which some gain pleasure while others feel defiled (violated).

If you are masturbating and you have control over it, please stop, especially if you have a desire to get or stay married. If it is an addiction, please ask the Lord for deliverance although it may be a long and very painful process. By the time the Lord is finished breaking all the chains, there will be no desire to do it again because you will realize the depth of the bondage you were under.

Some married couples are not enjoying sexual intimacy, with each other, as often as possible because one are both spouses are engaging in masturbation. Some couples have not shared sexual intimacy in a long time because one person is seemingly faithful and happy with abstaining, while the other is not. The unhappy spouse could hire a private detective who would not find any evidence of an affair, simply because another person is not involved.

If I could go back in time, I think I would go back to the sexual education class in the 7th grade. That was when the teacher taught us about masturbation, and sexual dreams, without teaching us of the potential spiritual implications and consequences. Please, do not masturbate... I know some people, especially Christians, will not believe some of the things I was inspired to share. On the contrary, for others, it will explain exactly what they have been going through. Even though some have never masturbated, or, may have even stopped a long time ago and no longer have a desire to do so. Unfortunately, devils are worse than a possessive ex who does not want to accept the fact that the former relationship is over. In addition, out of desperation, [the devil] is trying to do anything and everything possible to get back into or stay in your life. This may have seemed like a lot, but I could write a book on this topic.

Social Aloe Ministries: "Glorifying God. Exposing the devil."

In a sense, this is a book about masturbation, which is an act of either knowingly or unknowingly making a sacrifice unto the devil. There are several reasons why the Lord likens idolatry to spiritual adultery, and He uses scathing language against it. The Lord said, 'And *they shall no more offer their sacrifices unto devils, after whom they have gone a whoring. This shall be a statute for ever unto them throughout their generations.*' ~ Leviticus 17:7. You may not be familiar with the term "spirit spouse", or the names Succubus and Incubus. Well, a spirit spouse is an impure spirit that tries to enter into a covenantal relationship with a person, which the Lord forbids (Matthew 22:30). They are spiritual harlots and robbers. Regardless of whether a person willingly or unwillingly, knowingly or unknowingly enters into this union, the spirit is possessive and aggressive. It vigorously defends its perceived or proclaimed territory, which includes trying to block the person from reaching his or her God-ordained destiny, especially marriage. I will not go in depth about spirit spouses, in part because others have presented information on them. However, an **evil spirit trying to be a spouse played a part in my tribulation.**

The impure spirit attached itself to me and robbed me of blessings, things I had been unknowingly consenting to, such as when I initially started having sexual dreams without rebuking them and renouncing the covenants they formed. Anyone who has frequent or periodic dreams of a sexual nature has a spirit spouse whom they should divorce and fight to keep out of their life. Masturbation, pornography, fornication or adultery, and prostitution are some of the "legal" gateways we can open to these spirits. They can also enter "illegally" through sexual assault, rape, dreams or visions with sexual activity or being in water. Water!? What in the world does water have to do with a "spirit spouse"? I did not believe it when I first heard the devil's "marine kingdom". However, devils eventually show their hands. I know of satan's marine kingdom based on numerous personal encounters.

I love having a Scriptural reference for things: Book, chapter, and verse. However, the term "Holy Trinity" is not specifically used in the Bible and neither is "spirit spouse". Yet, please note, before the Lord used the flood to purge the earth, some of the angels engaged in the following activities that incurred the Lord's wrath:

> "And it came to pass, when men began to multiply on the face of the earth, and daughters were born unto them, that the sons of God saw the daughters of men that they were fair; and they took them wives of all which they chose." ~ Genesis 6:1-2

Please do not confuse the term "sons of God" with Jesus, the only begotten Son of God. Some minsters have preached that "sons of God" refer to human men, which I vehemently disagree with. For starters, it is written, "Now there was a day when THE SONS OF GOD came to present themselves before the Lord, and satan came also among them." ~ Job 1:6. The same term is also used prior to Job's second affliction (Job

2:1). By the way, **ministers may struggle with casting out a devil if the Lord is allowing it to stay for a period of time because the person is going through a trial like Job. Consequently, never assume a person who went through deliverance, got free, but returned with the same spirit is living in sin. Deliverance ministry is not a ministry based on assumptions.** Be careful to not condemn a righteous but afflicted person in a similar way like Job's friends, who wrongfully accused him of unrighteousness. The truth was far from it. They were unaware that the devil had been roaming around the earth during that time, like a busybody, looking to cause trouble. In addition, it was "…the Lord who said unto satan, *'Hast thou considered My servant Job, that there is none like him in the earth, a perfect and an upright man, one that feareth God, and escheweth evil?'"* ~ Job 1:8. Contrary to their belief, Job's persecution was a result of his righteousness. In the end, they needed Job more than he needed them:

> "And it was so, that after the Lord had spoken these Words unto Job, the Lord said to Eliphaz the Temanite, *My wrath is kindled against thee, and against thy two friends: for ye have not spoken of Me the thing that is right, as My servant Job hath. Therefore take unto you now seven bullocks and seven rams, and go to My servant Job, and offer up for yourselves a burnt offering; and My servant Job shall pray for you: for him will I accept: lest I deal with you after your folly, in that ye have not spoken of Me the thing which is right, like My servant Job.'*
>
> So Eliphaz the Temanite and Bildad the Shuhite and Zophar the Naamathite went, and did according as the Lord commanded them: the Lord also accepted Job. And the Lord turned the captivity of Job, when he prayed for his friends: also the Lord gave Job twice as much as he had before." ~ Job 42:7-10

The Lord allowed me to endure things in part so I can share a testimony based on firsthand information. He knew I would not hesitate to share my experiences. In fact, during my afflictions, I begged the Lord for opportunities to share my testimony. I wanted to expose the devil and help bring destruction to his kingdom. I was, and still am, fueled by a desire to repay him for what he has done to so many people, most of whom are ignorant of the devil's devices. Most importantly, I wanted to share this testimony, even if I look like a fool, for the glory of God. Isaiah had to walk around naked and barefoot for the Lord for three years as a prophetic sign (Isaiah 20). I prefer to expose things in this manner for all to see. I must warn people about how horrible hell must be, to provide hope for those who are suffering, and to let others know of the dangers of sexual immorality.

Some people are having sexual dreams about their God-ordained spouse, who is available to them in bed, but are unaware of how the enemy is using those encounters to covertly insert a third party into their union. In time, that evil spirit will sow seeds of marital discord, and some marriages ended because a "spirit spouse" destroyed it. Conversely, people are not getting married because a spirit is repelling potential suitors, especially those who cannot discern the spiritual enemy. Heartbreakingly, some people enjoy their "spiritual spouse" and say it is the best sex ever, either because they are clueless or willing to ignore how defiling such activities are. Other people are afraid to go to sleep because they get sexually assaulted every time they go to sleep. In some cases, people wake up in pain from the brutality of the sexual act. Some people are exhausted from sleep deprivation because they dread going to sleep, while others are worn down from marathon sexual encounters. Either way, the lack of rest opens the person up to a variety of illnesses. Sadly, whether it feels like making passionate love or being raped, the defiling consequences of spiritual sex are the same. In addition, the spirit is forging or maintaining a covenant and it sees even a Christian as its property, even though Jesus shed His blood for that son or daughter. The spirit becomes more possessive and stubborn based on the length of the "relationship". Consequently, it may require more praying, fasting, and deliverance sessions to permanently unseat it. However, please note, that type of a spirit is a stalker that will look for a way back into a person's life, which serves as an incentive to live a life of holiness.

So, do you still believe a Christian cannot have a demon? I dare you to publicly ask the members of your church about who has dreams of a sexual nature… Some things come down to semantics, so please consider these qualifying remarks. While some demons dwell in a person, others remain on the outside, like when the devil deceived Eve in the Garden of Eden. In the latter case, you cannot cast that demon out a person. In addition, a demon on the outside of a person can simply stay away when the person goes in for deliverance, which is a part of why **the Holy Spirit must guide ministers who are administering for deliverance**. For example, a Christian may not have a demon dwelling within, but there is a demon assigned to that person. The person may be able to discern how the spirit uses others for evil. A witch for example may have sent the impure spirit to monitor a person he or she desires to be in a relationship with or is trying to destroy. In case of the former, the impure spirit may try to seduce or even torment someone into entering a relationship with the witch. The spirit may also manipulate the witch into thinking the person wants a relationship, even at the cost of ignoring obvious rejection. This is one way of furthering the devil's objective of ensnaring the witch by luring him or her deeper into the occult. The impure spirit may try to ruin both people's lives by getting them into a miserable relationship, such as a marriage that will end in an embarrassing divorce, or better yet (from the devil's perspective) a union that ends in a murder-suicide. Therefore, the spirit gains advancement in the kingdom of darkness for getting two souls into hell.

A slight twist to the "spirit spouse" fiasco is it is not always a demon. It may be a human who engages in the occult and does what is called astral projection or soul travel. Some people have experienced the horrors of being stalked, whether physically or in cyberspace. Being spiritually stalked takes things to another level, and most law enforcement agencies would think you are nuts for reporting that a person's spirit is stalking you. This is a part of why a spirit may not dwell in a Christian.

Once I realized the sexual dreams were demonic, I began fighting against them in earnest. In keeping with the aforementioned jujitsu theme, it is easier to defend against certain moves before your opponent can really "sink them in". For example, there comes a point where it is too late to escape from a guillotine choke. Likewise, the familiar spirit who had invaded my life was firmly entrenched and was very reluctant to go. It was similar to someone you were in a relationship with, possibly a marriage, who does not want to accept the fact that the relationship is and has been over. You may have taken your wedding ring to a pawnshop while that person takes his or her wedding rings to the jeweler to get it cleaned periodically. You can basically cast out a "spirit spouse" one minute and it will try to come back into your life the next minute. You can go through deliverance, go to sleep and have a dream 20 minutes later with you hugging your mother. Sadly, the hug represents a covenant with the "spirit spouse", masquerading as your mother, to regain your acceptance. It is like getting divorced and going home to see your former spouse in your house, acting as if the two of you are still married…

We have only so far explored the tip of the iceberg. Things are about to get worse, even to the point where I asked the Lord to kill me and I meant it. Then I discovered that was exactly what the Lord was doing to me, killing the old me to make me a new creation in Christ Jesus. Someone commented on my humility and I basically said the Lord has humbled me.

The third chapter of "So, You Want to be a Prophet… ARE YOU CRAZY?" speaks of a third woman, a witch masquerading as a prophetess of the Lord. The one who said I was her God-ordained husband. When she "prophesied" that the Lord had selected the second lady as my wife, the one He said was His daughter. At that point, several things made sense, as if the veil had been lifted. However, Acts 16:16-18, tells of a lady who worked with a familiar spirit, a spirit of divination, who proclaimed the truth about Paul and Silas. But you do not ever want to come into agreement with an impure spirit, even if it tells you the truth. For as the Lord warned, *'Regard not them that have familiar spirits, neither seek after wizards, to be defiled by them: I AM the Lord your God.'* ~ Leviticus 19:31. Therefore, do not accept prophecies from everyone, even if the person is correct (Deuteronomy 13:1-5). Accepting a prophecy may put you in subjection to the god they are (truly) serving. The devil will use the truth as bait. The devil has hooked many people with the truth because they feel every subsequent revelation will also be true. It is like a false prophet who gives a revelation, as if it were a word of knowledge from God, such as a person's home address. In instances where the information is correct, someone may assume the subsequent prediction and associated instructions are also true… Once I came into agreement with that prophecy, I opened up a window to the enemy that he rapidly exploited.

After the witch "prophesied" to me, I began having weird dreams and visions. In one instance, I dreamt about the Lord's daughter, but she had an oversized forehead that was almost the size of a pumpkin. The enemy was trying to thwart my view of her in an attempt to make her less physically attractive, even though the source of my attraction was not physical. Correspondingly, in October 2015, the devil gave me a vision of the witch, without her large facial warts to make me find her attractive. By November 2015 the Lord revealed she was false and I was to disassociate myself from her, and her cohorts. I had moved on with my life, or so I thought, but she showed up in my dreams, either as herself or disguised as someone else. In one dream, she looked like the Lord's daughter. I thought it was strange when the Lord's daughter took me by my hand and was leading me somewhere, but then began huffing and puffing like someone who was out of shape. The Lord used other things to reveal the person in the dream was an imposter.

The dreams may have seemed like dreams from my soul based on the woman stalking and cyberstalking me, but they were sinister. I felt as if I needed deliverance and a minister of international renown came to my town in the summer of 2016. I still did not know what I was dealing with. Moreover, I had a dream on the morning I was going to have a deliverance session. I dreamt the witch's spirit was on the other side of the door leading to my garage, trying to prevent me from leaving my house. Within hours, it was revealed that she had tried to prevent me from getting delivered from a spirit of witchcraft, that she had sent. Mind you, this spirit came from a professing minister of Christ. Shockingly, the deliverance minister returned in 2017, and I got delivered from a spirit of witchcraft again, from the same witch. Later, in November 2017, the witch, after I banned her via at least 10 other fake Facebook accounts, posted a comment on one of my pages, which yielded a sharp public rebuke. That was when things truly got dark. The Lord used the declining situation to show how the enemy gets people into further bondage to him. The witch was embarrassed because she lied and said I was her God-ordained husband, but I wanted nothing to do with her. She was so sure the devil was going to offer her solutions, for a price.

On November 9, 2017, a woman showed up in my dream. The Lord let me know she was a voodoo priestess. Sadly, I was too slow to properly react so she released a spirit towards me before I could speak. A side effect of that attack has been sleep disturbance. By January 19, 2018, I had been through enough to upload a video teaching called "Signs & Symptoms of Witchcraft Attacks" to my Social Aloe Ministries YouTube channel. Shortly afterwards, I dreamt about the witch, and I rebuked her in the dream, which felt great. A few days later, she commented on that video, claiming to be my God-ordained wife and pastor. You may recall me saying I cut her loose in 2015, almost three years ago. Why was she still trying to be in my life, especially after the Lord exposed her true colors? I warned you that you would find some things hard to fathom, utterly perplexing. One of those things is this woman, whom I disassociated myself from, blocked from every social media outlet, publicly renounced, was contacting me about the same nonsense. I rebuked her again, based on the dream, and things got even worse. I had been calling a Blogtalk Radio show for deliverance from another deliverance minister of international renown. Despondently, I called the minister, received deliverance, I felt great for about three days, but the spirit reentered through a dream or vision where something happened against my will.

The enemy started fighting back once I started going through deliverance. I started hearing noises in my house, from a poltergeist (German for "noisy ghost", which is actually a devil or person engaging in astral projection). I also started having a weird sensation in the lower left quadrant of my abdomen, as if something was moving in it. I went through a deliverance session where I began to shake, my eyes turn beet red, and I started feeling like a snake was moving in my abdomen. The minister cast the devil out and I felt it leave my body through my mouth. In addition, the Lord allowed me to experience something to confirm it was for real. I tasted the demon as it left my body. When you exhale on cold winter day, you can see the frost leave your mouth, but it usually tastes fresh. I did not see the devil leave on that day, but I tasted a smoke that was like rotten eggs, something from the pits of hell. When you even decide to get deliverance, you are trying to unseat an enemy who does not want to leave until it destroys you. It also hates you and wants to exploit every loophole possible to stay in or return to your life. It does not like surrendering the territory it felt like it worked hard to get. I later realized the correlation between how the witch was acting in an obsessive manner, claiming she was my wife when evidence indicates otherwise, the spirit acting like I belonged to the devil instead of Jesus. Also, the spirit would never try to put me with the Lord's daughter, but it tried to put me with a daughter of the devil.

The Lord used to give me at least one dream per night, even though it would have three to six transitions, all of which had different interpretations. But somewhere along the line, my dreams and visions about the Lord's plans shifted to those about the devil's plans. It was like the devil was flooding me with junk mail so I would not receive anything from the Lord. Reasons for this strategy from the devil include:

- Torment me so I would ask the Lord to take away my visionary gifts and/or quit the ministry.
- Cause me to lose faith in my ability to discern the source of a dream or vision, thereby potentially rejecting all future dreams and visions as being demonic.
- Induce a spirit of fear because of the sexual assaults, nightmares, and demonic visitations while I slept.
- Discourage me from breaking the enemy's yokes through Christ Jesus by fasting and praying.
- Lead me to believe my efforts to obtain deliverance were not working, and that the Lord was weak and had abandoned me.
- Instill doubt that the Word of God, the Bible, was true. For example, James 4:7 states, "Submit yourselves therefore to God. Resist the devil, and he will flee from you." Yet, despite submitting to the Lord, and vigorously resisting the devil, he was not fleeing. The enemy also had an agenda to lead me to the wrong woman, which included trying to make it seem as if the attacks were continuing because I was not fully submitting to the Lord by choosing the woman He had chosen for me.
- Doubt the Lord's promise to give me victory this year.
- Make me believe the Lord does not love me, despite what is written in John 3:16, and how Jesus atoned for my sins on the cross.
- Motivate me to kill the witch and her family and/or commit suicide. The devil presented death as my only solution to gain freedom.
- Seduce or force me to work for him, but I will not work for that loser, one who is selfish and void of any love
- Doubt my salvation that comes only from Jesus's sacrifice on the cross.

- Surround me with darkness until darkness was all I could see.
- Kill my prayer and worship life.
- Distract me with warfare in an effort to reduce the time I spent studying the Scriptures.
- Get me to hate God, to curse Him and die.

I oftentimes wondered what the devil had seen in me to dedicate so much time, effort, and other precious resources in an effort to stop me. I seriously considered this an overkill. I am reminded of two additional Scriptures I clung to like a life raft during this tumultuous season:

- "But the more they afflicted them, the more they multiplied and grew. And they were grieved because of the children of Israel." ~ Exodus 1:12
- "It is good for me that I have been afflicted; that I might learn Thy statutes." ~ Psalm 119:71

CHAPTER 3

TO HELL, AND BACK

"According to their deeds, accordingly He will repay, fury to His adversaries, recompence to His enemies; to the islands He will repay recompence. So shall they fear the name of the Lord from the west, and His glory from the rising of the sun. **When the enemy shall come in like a flood, the Spirit of the Lord shall lift up a standard against him.**"
Isaiah 59:18-19

Some people pretend as if the Lord did not allow the devil to afflict Job, even though the Scripture clearly says so (Job 1-2). It foreshadowed how, shortly after Jesus' baptism, "Then was **Jesus led up of the Spirit into the wilderness to be tempted of the devil.**" ~ Matthew 4:1. One thing both men had in common was the Heavenly Father allowed the devil to afflict them, BECAUSE of their righteousness. Would you still love and honor the Lord if He handed you over to the tormentors for a season, or, would you curse Him? During his tribulation, Job, speaking of the Lord, said, *'Though He slay me, yet will I trust in Him...'* ~ Job 13:15a. Will you trust the Lord while He is slaying you?

I do not put myself on par with Job, and especially with Jesus, but I can empathize with being handed over to the tormentors, even though I was not living in sin. I call it going through hell on earth, and I had to go through it in order to get to the other side. That was what Jesus endured in the wilderness before the angels ministered unto Him after His trial was over (Matthew 4:11). By God's grace, I endured the enemy's attacks, which only had a few strategic themes, but with seemingly endless diversities in each area. Based on the leading of the Holy Spirit, here are several samples of these types of attacks.

Sleep Deprivation

I began experiencing severe sleep deprivation in November 2017, which was meant to wear me down and make me succumb to the witch (devil). Oh, I almost forgot about the Lord revealing that the witch was trying to make me sick to the point where she would get the chance to take care of me. That demonic logic was sick within itself. It also illustrates how desperate some people are for a relationship, even with someone who does not like or even hates them. Unexpectedly at the time, the attacks became more overt and intense when I started going through deliverance in January 2018. Prior to that, I knew an impure spirit was in my home, but mostly watching, quietly. Then it became a noisy devil (a poltergeist) in an effort to torment me.

There are different ways to discern demonic presence. The Lord may allow you to see the demon, which makes it very obvious or you may see it looking like a monster, an animal or human, or as a dark or white shadow. Temperature changes in a portion or entire room; it may get either very hot or very cold. I went through attacks while I slept where I woke up sweating. You may also get "the creeps", an eerie feeling coupled with the hairs on the back of your neck standing up or getting the chills. Demons are also perceptible by smell, as are human spirits. A demon's odor may vary based on the demon and/or its mood. I recall smelling burning wood, which, during the winter made it seemed like smoke from a neighbor's chimney. There were times after a major victory when the devil return and I smelled its anger. It tried filling the house with hate and anger, but darkness cannot overcome Light. The smoky smell even intensified at times to smell like fire. A devil getting angry with me is laughable because it means I am pleasing the Lord. Another devil smelled like pineapple upside down cake. I did not care how good it smelled because Ephesians 5:11 states, **"...have**

no fellowship with the unfruitful works of darkness, but rather reprove them." I hate devils, especially stubborn ones who either refuse to leave or keep coming back. There are also times when demons move or steal things. And of course, demons talk.

I recall being in my office downstairs and my house was peaceful, just like how I love and want it. Then I heard a loud thud, as if a parachutist landed in my bedroom. And just in case I thought it was nothing, the devil disturbed my peace by making noises as it moved around the house. One such noise was a clicking sound. Sometimes I ran upstairs to immediately confront the demon. Other times, I was simply too busy, and since a part of the devil's function was to consume my time, I kept working. I also heard a clicking sound, like someone clipping his or her fingernails. It was almost hilarious how petty the devil was. The spirit acted like a spouse who responded in a way that meant he/she was not getting the desired attention by making noises around the house, so I let the devil suffer in its own shenanigans.

I spent a lot of time in spiritual warfare prayer one night. Shortly afterwards, the spirit startled me by intentionally pressing down on the floorboard, which made a few loud creaking noises. In addition to trying to induce fear, it was letting me know it had not left, was not leaving, and did not have to leave, regardless of which Jesus I was calling on. That was a part of why I did not always confront the demons. I felt it was pointless at times if the Lord was not making them leave. Initially, it was perplexing why the devils were trampling all over the name and shed blood of Christ Jesus. After all, the Bible says, "Thou believest that there is one God; thou doest well: the devils also believe, and tremble." ~ James 2:19. I knew if the devils were not trembling now, they would eventually. The "free shots" they were getting to take against me were going to cost them dearly when they faced the Lord:

> "Let God arise, let His enemies be scattered: let them also that hate Him flee before Him. As smoke is driven away, so drive them away: as wax melteth before the fire, so let the wicked perish at the presence of God. But let the righteous be glad; let them rejoice before God: yea, let them exceedingly rejoice." ~ Psalm 68:1-3

A young man testified of the Lord delivering him from demonic oppression because of his father's prayers. He had a visitation from a dark shadowy figure one night, but then another entity showed up, a person dressed in bright white. As soon as the devil saw the other figure, it took off running and never returned. I kept wondering when the Lord was going to show up for me like that. I had been fasting and praying for almost a year, begging the Lord to arise so the enemy would scatter from my life

People tend to have a bad attitude when they are sleep deprived. Prolonged periods of sleep deprivation wears down the body and opens a person up to illnesses, such as adrenal fatigue from being in a state of "fright or flight". In addition, sleep deprived people do not usually make good decisions. Among many things, depriving me of sleep was meant to convince me I was out of the Lord's will, and, I would not have any peace until I obeyed Him. By the way, that is reflective of a person's thought pattern when praying witchcraft prayers. It is a form of witchcraft to ask the Lord to not to allow a person to rest until he or she does something, especially to meet a selfish agenda, one that violates a person's free will. Those prayers may conjure and release devils to torment the targeted individual, particularly if they violate the Lord's will for the person. It is truly wise to not hastily come into agreement with another person's prayer request, even one that seems righteous. An example is prayer to restore a marriage. God hates divorce, but it may not have been His will for those individuals to get married in the first place. In addition, He knows of the looming disaster if they had stayed together. Some people have either ignorantly or arrogantly prayed such prayers and the targeted individual succumbed to the demonic pressure, got back into the marriage, that is followed by that person's death. Be very careful about getting involved in witchcraft, to include by praying ungodly prayers. Even such an innocent act opens you and your family, down to the third and fourth generation, to demonic entities. Matthew 1:18-25 shows how the Lord maintains or restores a relationship by providing peace, Godly peace from the Prince of Peace, Jesus.

I told the demon that was afflicting me it should have left the first time I commanded it to leave in the name of Jesus. I asked the Lord to make this a part of its punishment. Have the demon return and say to the devil, 800 times, "Jesus is Lord!" I chose the number 800 because if you plant a kernel of corn it will produce a stalk with an average of 800 kernels. The demon will reap what it has sown, abundantly. When it spends eternity suffering in the lake of fire, I want it to remember that it should have left me alone, the first time. As I close this section, I heard that sleep deprivation is one of the worst torture devices. That is not a good thing when facing an enemy who does not sleep and has nothing better to do than to torture people.

Demonic Encounters

The devil launched a series of persistent attacks against me in the form of dreams, visions, and visitations, some of which were not readily apparent as being demonic. Sadly, there is division amongst believers in Christ Jesus that is interwoven into but also transcends into denominational lines. That critical line exists between those who are classified as being cessationists and the hyper-charismatics.

Cessationists basically believe that the gifts of the Holy Spirit the apostle Paul was inspired to write about, which establishes the doctrine for the New Testament church, are no longer in operation. For some reason, which I have never heard articulated in a way without contradicting Scriptures, cessationists believe the gifts of the Holy Spirit ceased after the (original) apostles passed away. Cessationists also believe that even though the saints have not been perfected, of the five ministry gifts listed in Ephesians 4:11, apostles and prophets no longer exist. A part of their rationale is because an apostle must have been a part of Jesus's earthly ministry. This is based on a requirement used to select Matthias, the person who replaced Judas (Acts 1:15-26). Some say Matthias was the last apostle, even though the Bible clearly says Barnabas and Paul were apostles (Acts 14:14). If Paul was not an apostle, much of what we call the New Testament is invalid because they came through him. In addition, it defies the cessationist theology that being an apostle means having been a part of Jesus's earthly ministry. Paul (Saul) was too busy as a Pharisee, studying under the famous doctor of the Law, Gamaliel, to follow Jesus. In fact, Paul gained his apostleship after a direct encounter with the resurrected Christ Jesus. **Is it possible, that Jesus, who is the same yesterday, today, and forevermore, can still call people to serve Him, even as apostles, similarly to how He called Paul?**

Again, for the cessationists who believe an apostle must have been a part of Jesus's earthly ministry, Paul creates a problem. They either have to believe he is an apostle or not. If he was not an apostle, several books of the Bible were erroneously canonized. If he was an apostle, how can being an apostle of Christ require having spent time as a part of His earthly ministry? Interestingly, Paul chronicled his apostolic journey in a way, that at least some people would believe, sets a precedent for the Lord calling other people as His apostles or prophets if He so desires:

> "For do I now persuade men, or God? Or do I seek to please men? For if I yet pleased men, I should not be the servant of Christ. But I certify you, brethren, that the gospel which was preached of me is not after man. For I neither received it of man, neither was I taught it, but by the revelation of Jesus Christ. For ye have heard of my conversation in time past in the Jews' religion, how that beyond measure I persecuted the church of God, and wasted it: And profited in the Jews' religion above many my equals in mine own nation, being more exceedingly zealous of the traditions of my fathers. But when it pleased God, who separated me from my mother's womb, and called me by His grace, To reveal His Son in me, that I might preach Him among the heathen; immediately I conferred not with flesh and blood: Neither went I up to Jerusalem to them which were apostles before me; but I went into Arabia, and returned again unto Damascus.
>
> Then after three years I went up to Jerusalem to see Peter, and abode with him fifteen days. But other of the apostles saw I none, save James the Lord's brother. Now the things which I write unto you, behold, before God, I lie not. Afterwards I came into the regions of Syria and Cilicia; And was unknown by face unto the churches of Judaea which were in Christ: But they had heard only, that he which persecuted us in times past now preacheth the faith which once he destroyed. And they glorified God in me." ~ Galatians 1:10-24

There are potentially negative impacts to trying to prove your calling to people. Consider Jesus, who, despite His many wonderful works, could not convince some people, even after His death and resurrection, that He was (and still is) the Son of God. Some people refer to Paul as a self-appointed apostle, just like any current professing apostle or prophet. **Interestingly,**

people do not usually call someone a self-appointed pastor. Yet, a person can become a pastor by going to a seminary, without a calling from the Lord. The original 12 apostles, oftentimes called the "Apostles of the Lamb", were a part of Jesus's earthly ministry. The apostle James, Jesus' brother, was not among the 12 (Matthew 10:2-5). There was even a time when Jesus was ministering and His family and friends thought He had lost His mind. As a result, Mary showed up with His brothers (presumably including James) and sisters, in opposition to Jesus' earthly ministry (Mark 3). Yet, James, brother of Christ, became an apostle, even though he was NOT a part of his brother's earthly ministry (Galatians 1:19).

Despite Ephesians 4:1-16, cessationists also argue against the existence of prophets, because it is written, "God, who at sundry times and in divers manners spake in time past unto the fathers by the prophets, hath in these last days spoken unto us by His Son, whom He hath appointed heir of all things, by whom also He made the worlds." ~ Hebrews 1:1-2. But one of the ways to look at this is how the president of the United States speaks on behalf of the nation. But the president also has ambassadors to various nations, and even to the United Nations, that speak on behalf of the president of the United States. Tragically, many people who cite Hebrews 1:1-2 will not listen to prophets because they will not listen to Jesus. After all, Jesus said, *'He that heareth you heareth Me; and he that despiseth you despiseth Me; and he that despiseth Me despiseth Him that sent Me.'* ~ Luke 10:19. Being labeled as "self-appointed" is nothing new. We see how the Lord called Jeremiah to serve Him (Jeremiah 1). It was a private one-on-one event, and even thought he was a prophet of the Lord to the nations, and internationally recognized as a prophet today, he was called "self-appointed" back then: *'Now therefore why hast thou not reproved Jeremiah of Anathoth, which maketh himself a prophet to you?'* ~ Jeremiah 29:27

Cessationists firmly believe the Lord no longer communicates to us outside of Scriptures, hence "Sola Scriptura". Sadly, sometimes the Bible is not enough to convince a cessationist to change a belief. Based on "Sola Scriptura", if you do not have a Bible, or access to someone who knows the Word of the Lord, you will never hear from the Lord directly. This contradicts what Peter said, which was in accordance with Joel 2:28-32:

"But Peter, standing up with the eleven, lifted up his voice, and said unto them, *'Ye men of Judaea, and all ye that dwell at Jerusalem, be this known unto you, and hearken to my words: For these are not drunken, as ye suppose, seeing it is but the third hour of the day. But this is that which was spoken by the prophet Joel; 'And it shall come to pass in the last days', saith God, 'I will pour out of My Spirit upon all flesh: and your sons and your daughters shall prophesy, and your young men shall see visions, and your old men shall dream dreams: And on My servants and on My handmaidens I will pour out in those days of My Spirit; and they shall prophesy: And I will shew wonders in heaven above, and signs in the earth beneath; blood, and fire, and vapour of smoke: The sun shall be turned into darkness, and the moon into blood, before the great and notable day of the Lord come: And it shall come to pass, that whosoever shall call on the name of the Lord shall be saved."* ~ Acts 2:14-21

A part of that theology is because, apparently, everything the Lord needs to say is already in the Scriptures. Any new revelation is viewed as extra biblical, which would require reopening the canon. However, receiving a new revelation does not necessitate reopening the canon. For example, every revelation during the time of Jesus's earthly ministry did not make it into the Bible. John clearly wrote, "And there are also many other things which Jesus did, the which, if they should be written every one, I suppose that even **the world itself could not contain the books that should be written**. Amen." ~ John 21:25. One person who knows of everything Jesus did is the Holy Spirit. We also see how the Lord revealed things to Daniel that he was not allowed to disclose (Daniel 12:9). Likewise, the apostle John (Revelation 10:4) received revelations he was not even authorized to record. In addition, the Book of Obadiah only has one chapter, but it does not mean that is the only prophetic utterance he ever received from the Lord. There are also prophecies that were spoken without being recorded. It therefore seems reasonable to me that the Lord has not gone silent simply because we have the Bible. After all, the Holy Spirit is still here.

An alleged communication from the Lord does not mean we need to reopen and revise the Scriptures. Most of the prophets of the Lord in the Bible are unnamed. We do not even know what most of their prophecies were about. Every revelation from the Lord did not go in the Bible back then, and the same applies today. I have heard about people who came to salvation because of an encounter they say was with Christ Jesus in a dream or vision. Should we tell the former Muslim or witch that they were imagining things and they need to return to their former practices until a human preaches the gospel of Christ Jesus to them?

Cessationists discredit the ministries of professing apostles and prophets by calling them "self-appointed" or false. The premise of "So, You Want to be a Prophet… ARE YOU CRAZY?" is no one in his or her right mind wants to be a prophet, or an apostle. The spiritual warfare that comes from other professing Christians is enough to make a professing apostle or prophet quit the ministry. Paul, the apostle, also gave the following accounts to make anyone think long and hard about wanting those positions:

> "And what shall I more say? For the time would fail me to tell of Gedeon, and of Barak, and of Samson, and of Jephthae; of David also, and Samuel, and of the prophets:
>
> Who through faith subdued kingdoms, wrought righteousness, obtained promises, stopped the mouths of lions. Quenched the violence of fire, escaped the edge of the sword, out of weakness were made strong, waxed valiant in fight, turned to flight the armies of the aliens. Women received their dead raised to life again: and others were tortured, not accepting deliverance; that they might obtain a better resurrection: And others had trial of cruel mockings and scourgings, yea, moreover of bonds and imprisonment: They were stoned, they were sawn asunder, were tempted, were slain with the sword: they wandered about in sheepskins and goatskins; being destitute, afflicted, tormented; (Of whom the world was not worthy:) they wandered in deserts, and in mountains, and in dens and caves of the earth. And these all, having obtained a good report through faith, received not the promise." ~ Hebrews 11:32-39

> "For I think that God hath set forth us the apostles last, as it were appointed to death: for we are made a spectacle unto the world, and to angels, and to men. We are fools for Christ's sake, but ye are wise in Christ; we are weak, but ye are strong; ye are honourable, but we are despised. Even unto this present hour we both hunger, and thirst, and are naked, and are buffeted, and have no certain

dwelling place; And labour, working with our own hands: being reviled, we bless; being persecuted, we suffer it: Being defamed, we intreat: we are made as the filth of the world, and are the offscouring of all things unto this day.

I write not these things to shame you, but as my beloved sons I warn you." ~ 1 Corinthians 4:9-17

Many ministers are called self-appointed as a way of creating a barrier that cannot be broken down by natural means. Based on Scriptures, the Lord oftentimes called people into prophetic ministry privately and directly. How can a person be a prophet without hearing directly from the Lord? The Lord called Moses as His prophet while he was tending sheep. The Bible does not say whether people were present to confirm the Lord had called Moses as His prophet. The men who witnessed Paul's encounter with Christ Jesus were in the dark about what truly happened, and about his commission. They could only attest to a bright light that left Saul blind, until the Lord commissioned Ananias to minister unto Saul (Acts 8-9). We also see how Samuel was a young man who ministered unto the Lord under the high priest Eli. Samuel did not even know the Lord's voice. But rather than going through Eli to tell him, the entire priesthood, and possibly the nation about Samuel's calling, the Lord went to Samuel directly and privately. Eli had to ask Samuel about what happened. In addition, this is how people found out Samuel had been called as a prophet of the Lord:

> "And Samuel grew, and the Lord was with him, and did let none of his words fall to the ground. And all Israel from Dan even to Beersheba knew that Samuel was established to be a prophet of the Lord." ~1 Samuel 3:19-20

The Lord also called Jeremiah as a young man, and this account speaks volumes to those with the ears to hear what the Spirit of the Lord is saying:

> Then the Word of the Lord came unto me, saying, *'Before I formed thee in the belly I knew thee; and before thou camest forth out of the womb I sanctified thee, and I ordained thee a prophet unto the nations.'*
>
> Then said I, *'Ah, Lord God! Behold, I cannot speak: for I am a child.'*
>
> But the Lord said unto me, *'Say not, I am a child: for thou shalt go to all*

> *that I shall send thee, and whatsoever I command thee thou shalt speak. Be not afraid of their faces: for I AM with thee to deliver thee'*, saith the Lord." ~ Jeremiah 1:4-8

Cessationists may want to also prayerfully consider:

> For through him we both have access by one Spirit unto the Father. Now therefore ye are no more strangers and foreigners, but fellow citizens with the saints, and of the household of God; **And are built upon the foundation of the apostles and prophets, Jesus Christ Himself being the Chief Corner Stone**; In whom all the building fitly framed together groweth unto an holy temple in the Lord: In whom ye also are builded together for an habitation of God through the Spirit." ~ Ephesians 2:18-22

If the Jesus Christ, the Chief Cornerstone, has not been removed from the church, why should the foundation of the apostles and prophets? But then again, some churches have managed to push Jesus out. For those who seemingly have not, but have dismissed the apostles and prophets, when you remove the foundation, the structure inevitably and eventually crumbles.

While cessationists (seemingly) do not believe anything that is not specified in the Bible, hyper-charismatics have tremendous faith to believe things that either seemingly have or are untethered from the safety of the Bible. The division between cessationists and hyper-charismatics reminds me of the Sadducees and the Pharisees. They both professed a belief in God, which is now debatable based on their lack of belief in Jesus, but "…the Sadducees say that there is no resurrection, neither angel, nor spirit: but the Pharisees confess both." ~ Acts 23:8. Yet, in a display of hypocrisy, it was a Sadducee who asked Jesus about a woman's marital status at the time of the resurrection (see Matthew 22:23-32).

Hyper-charismatics believe in the "Five-Fold Ministry" listed in Ephesians 4:11, and the current operation of the gifts of the Holy Spirit featured in 1 Corinthians 12. Sadly, sometimes those beliefs contradict sound Biblical doctrine. For example, some things are linked to the Holy Spirit because they seem like gifts of the Holy Spirit, even though they lack the fruit of the Spirit (Galatians 5:22-23). They consider people with a long history of false prophecies as prophets of the Lord. Some claim New Testament prophets do not have to be accurate, or as accurate as Old Testament prophets. If you have seen the list of my published works, or read them, to include the blog and other social media posts, you know how I feel about the current application of Ephesians 4:11. Likewise, you will also know how I feel about Deuteronomy 13:1-5 and 18:20-22. I do not play with God's grace, and more so than ever, especially after writing this book, I will not trample on Jesus's shed blood.

Somewhere between cessationism and hyper-charismata is sound Biblical doctrine that does not impede or diminish the functions of the Holy Spirit, or grieve or quench Him. **I believe Jesus when He said the Holy Spirit would show us things to come, which qualifies as revelation, or dare I say, extra-biblical revelation (John 16:13).** I also believe the entire Bible, from Genesis to Revelation, even though some of the words are not the Word of God. Before you start shouting blasphemy, remember the words of the devil, such as Genesis 3, Job 1-2, Isaiah 14:12-18, Luke 4:1-13, etc. The Scriptures are closed but the devil is still speaking and leading people astray, which means now is certainly not the time for the Lord to remain silent. However, revelations from the Lord must be rooted in Scriptures, either based on how He communicated with others, such as Jeremiah at the potter's house (Jeremiah 18), or, because He quotes Scriptures as a part of an "extra-biblical" revelation. For example, in one of the many times the Lord has communicated directly to me, He quoted a part of Joel 2:25 by saying, *"I will restore unto you the years the locust has eaten."* That promise directly from the Lord has been a tremendous source of strength duty this trial, because, like Job, the Lord will restore everything the devil has thought he has stolen, killed, or destroyed. My faith is in my Lord, my God.

"Then said Jesus to them again, *'Peace be unto you: as My Father hath sent Me, even so send I you.'* And when He had said this, He breathed on them, and saith unto them, *'Receive ye the Holy Ghost.'"* ~ John 20:21-22. The Holy Spirit later descended on the earth like a rushing mighty wind (Acts 2). There is a correlation between spirit and wind. When the Lord delivered me from a spirit of masturbation, the sneeze expelled the spirit, which felt like a puff of wind. Similarly, in deliverance sessions, I was delivered from spirits that were expelled via coughing or even yawning. It felt like a regular cough or yawn, coupled with other signs such as feeling lighter and/or being able to think clearer. There was a time when I tasted a spirit as it left, and it smelled like rotten eggs. The first time I went through a deliverance session I came home and slept like a baby. Please note that simply sneezing, coughing, or yawning do not automatically cleanse a person of an impure spirit. Spirits only leave because of the name and power of Jesus.

On the contrary, because it was "open season" on me, there were times when I inhaled and felt and/or saw a spirit enter me. One night I had a demonic visitation when I got stuck and could not move or speak ("sleep paralysis"). The fighter in me tried resisting, but I could not even move my head. The room was dark, but I saw the darker shadow of the impure spirit entering me, like smoke going back down a chimney. I was angry with the Lord for allowing it. How could a spirit just enter me like that, as if I were a child of the devil or living like one? Why wasn't the Lord protecting me from such brazen attacks? Why was I praying Psalm 91 where it says the Lord gives His angels charge over us, and, Psalm 127:2 where it says the Lord gives "…His beloved sleep"? Did God hate me so He left me defenseless against these devils? Also, forget about wanting to confront the devil, who is the angel or are the angels assigned to watch over me? I wanted to give that angel or those angels a piece of my mind. And lastly, how could I ever trust the Lord, especially to protect me after this? Despite those burning questions, I knew I was going to come out of with more gifts and a greater level of gifting from the Lord, and also more authority from the Lord especially over the very types of devils He was allowing to afflict me.

There were times when spirits entered me in dreams because I was around people who were smoking. Oddly, I do not smoke, and I despise the smell of cigarette smoke. When someone smokes around me, either I am leaving or that person is leaving. Yet in one dream, "I" let people blow cigarette smoke on me without doing or saying anything. Again, there were times when I was frustrated with the Lord for allowing the enemy to attack me in such ways, especially when things were happening that I would not do or allow in real life, which is a sign of sorcery. On that note, a part of being (more) sensitive to spiritual things, there were times throughout the day when I felt like things were being pumped into my nostrils. It was like an anesthesiologist putting on a mask to infuse a patient with anesthesia.

Sorcery was a part of why some things were happening while I slept. While devils can take actions independent of people, anyone who engages in sorcery is at enmity with God. Revelation 21:8 states that unrepentant sorcerers will spend eternity in the lake of fire. I knew the Lord was either going to use me to help lead people to repent, especially after seeing that despite my frustrations, I would not turn on Him and work for the devil. Their actions against me will instead contribute to their damnation and demise. In a similar way, the Lord allowed the Egyptians to afflict the Israelites for centuries until the iniquities of the Amorites came to its fullness (Genesis 15:13-16). It is never good for the enemy when the Lord allows him to afflict His children. The Lord eventually avenges His children and compensates them. The Israelites basically plundered Egypt. Is it odd how the Egyptians gave the Israelites things as they left. The Israelites borrowed things they would not return (Exodus 3:21-22, 11:1-3, and 12:35-36).

When the Lord led the Israelites into the Promised Land, they were to utterly destroy many things and make no covenants with the inhabitants of the land. I was eager to do my part to help destroy the enemy's kingdom, and partake of the plunder for all the suffering. I wanted to utterly destroy the enemy's kingdom, and despite the enemy's repeated and numerous attempts to forge covenants with me, there is no room in my life for devils. I call it "demonic logic" for devils to think they could try to make my life hell on earth, and think I would want to be in a covenant with them. My relationship with the enemy is strictly adversarial. As Jesus instructed, I forgive every person who partnered with devils in an effort to ruin my life. I have often interceded for them, and particularly their children, grandchildren, and actual or potential great grandchildren, all of whom they have brought serious curses upon. There is no need to curse those who have cursed themselves, and their families. That makes it even easier to forgive them. However, I will never forgive the devils. I want to destroy them.

That reminds me of another "sleep paralysis" attack where I saw a part of the demon on top of me. I am not sure if I called on the name of Jesus, but I was so angry that I bit the demon's leathery skin on its chest, then the attack ended. I hoped it sent a message that I was not giving up and would fight back with every Godly resource available to me. If the Lord was not going to give me the necessary support to prevent or defend against these attacks, I was going to do as much as possible by myself to fight back. Many soldiers have requested indirect fire or close air support during combat but did not receive it. Even though potentially angry with their higher command, they knew they must continue fighting, even to their death.

The Lord was not giving me the firepower and support I wanted and needed for a swift and decisive victory, which meant I had to use every available resource to fight. Many believers cannot fathom the concept of the Lord teaching us how to fight. We can learn a lot from studying the following:

> And Moses said unto the people, *'Fear ye not, stand still, and see the salvation of the Lord, which He will shew to you to day: for the Egyptians whom ye have seen to day, ye shall see them again no more for ever. The Lord shall fight for you, and ye shall hold your peace.'*
>
> And the Lord said unto Moses, ***'Wherefore criest thou unto Me?*** *Speak unto the children of Israel, that they go forward: But lift thou up thy rod, and stretch out thine hand over the sea, and divide it: and the children of Israel shall go on dry ground through the midst of the sea. And I, behold, I will harden the hearts of the Egyptians, and they shall follow them: and I will get Me honour upon Pharaoh, and upon all his host, upon his chariots, and upon his horsemen. And the Egyptians shall know that I AM the Lord, when I have gotten Me honour upon Pharaoh, upon his chariots, and upon his horsemen.'* ~ Exodus 14:13-18

The Lord may allow our backs to get pressed against the wall, like the Israelites by the Red Sea, before intervening. By the way, I find it humorous that the Lord asked Moses why he was crying out to Him. Yet, in this case, I wondered if I had something that I was not using against the enemy. In addition, please note how the Lord was going to provoke the enemy to pursue His children so He could destroy them. I salivated at the thought of the Lord ridding me of these stubborn spirits. In an extreme test of faith, such as with Lazarus, the Lord allows us to die to show He is the Resurrection.

Because spirits are air, and oftentimes entered and left while I breathed, there were times when I felt like I was being punished for the mere act of breathing. Sometimes my reaction after a demonic attack was to wonder if I had breathed wrong. It felt like I was being punished for everything, such as driving 1mph over the speed limit for even a second. **One of the good outcomes of the attacks was they taught me live uprightly.** I do not ever want the Lord to hand me over to the devil like that again, especially to spend an eternity living like that in hell. I do not ever want the devil to have or feel like he has the freedom to do with me as he pleases, whenever he pleases. Even though some of what I will share next demonstrate that I knew regardless of the demonic onslaught, the devil had to operate within the limits the Lord had established, as was in the case of Job. The angels were watching over me, not to my liking, but certainly in accordance with the Lord's will. That was why I even dared the enemy to kill me, because I know he could not. There was a point where I was so angry with the Lord that I threatened Him. I told the Lord He would not be able to hide from me because I was going to hunt Him down. Like the woman with the issue of blood (Luke 8:43-48), I was going to do what it took to reach Him but I was not going to let go. I was going to wrestle the Lord like Jacob until He blessed me (Genesis 32).

Homosexuality

Some demonic encounters were sexual in nature, to include those with a "spirit of homosexuality". One of the first encounters I can recall involved me standing, and a guy, whose face I could not see, came up behind me. It initially seemed like a friend sneaking up on another to give a friendly hug. I saw the events unfold from the right side. The spirit masqueraded as a body builder with muscular arms that easily stretched the measuring tape beyond 20 inches. I subsequently realized the gesture was not friendly. On the contrary, it was like a snake, trying to get close enough to me to get a hold and begin squeezing the life out of me. I responded quickly and got out of the hold and woke up. I did not give much thought to the dream or know how to handle it.

I had another encounter while sleeping on my right side. Oddly, I had the typical "sleep paralysis" symptoms, but I felt the spirit on my lower back. The incident made me feeling very vulnerable, as if I needed to sleep on my back. My house, my own bedroom, was no safer than a prison cell. I became leery of leaving my rear uncovered while I slept. I thought the spirit had fled until I went to a church and a minister was praying. She suddenly looked down at my lower abdomen while I was standing up. She did not want to get specific, but she commanded a spirit to come out of me in the name of Jesus. She later told me it was a spirit of homosexuality. Then it made sense why the spirit was on my lower back. Obviously, this was no way for a child of God to live especially with someone who was ministering for the Lord. To be brutally honest, I had an issue leading anyone to Christ if they were going to have to live like I was. Simultaneously, this made me realize that having a spirit of homosexuality does not make someone a homosexual, but it works on changing a person's sexual orientation. Like all demons, this spirit works on taking a person to hell for sexual perversion (Romans 1:24-32, Revelation 21:8, etc.).

Another thing of note was the minister also cast out a spirit of witchcraft. The minister knew of the woman professing to be my wife. The Lord used this encounter to reveal the woman was a liar who also engaged in the dark arts. But most notable, she was perplexed because I had a very powerful demon that was assigned to me, and only me. She recommended a minister with greater spiritual authority to deliver me. I did not know at the time, but the spirit she described was a type of familiar spirit called a "spirit spouse". It felt like a blessing that the recommended deliverance minister was coming to town within two weeks, at the Lord's daughter's church. I went to the church and she was not there and the minister did not deliver me.

Among many things, these attacks gave me a deeper understanding of how some people turn to same sex relationships. Some people engage in sexually perverse things in heterosexual relationships because impure spirits market them as being fun and adventurous. Demonically influenced people will even pretend to enjoy things they hate or may find painful to endure. The Lord ordained sex for married couples, but that does not include oral or anal sex. If you engage in anal sex with a man for example, and you begin to enjoy it more than vaginal sex, you are being set up by the devil. The devil slowly lured Eve to partake of the "forbidden fruit", and subsequently lead Adam into sin. It was a systematic process of getting her to look at it, question the Lord's words and motives for prohibiting it, and getting her to try it. If the devil can lead a man to have anal sex with a woman, he can get him to have anal sex with a man. One of the ways to bridge this chasm is when a man cross-dresses. I may have offended some people. But I am here to warn of the devil's devices, many of which he used on me, yet I know he has many more devices in his arsenal. For example, another potential precursor to homosexuality is masturbation. A man who masturbates is pleasuring a man, just like how a woman who masturbates is pleasuring a woman. The Lord implemented rules to protect us. **By the way, I prefer to offend people into heaven than to comfort them into hell.**

Attempted (Demonic) Rape

Thank the Lord that these encounters did not go as far as the devil would have liked. Demons have raped men and women, leaving them with signs and symptoms of being physically violated. Sometimes the predators are men and women who soul travel (astral projection). They may call their actions having sex but it is actually rape. Astral projection is both evil and dangerous for its practitioners. The Lord is more merciful than me because my motto is, "If it flies, it dies." I had encounters, to include dreams, where the witch sexually assaulted me. However, the focus of this section is on what devils do.

The last time a demon tried to rape me, I dreamt of a muscular Hispanic man wearing a yellow shirt and gray shorts. He came through my door and was creeping towards me in a strange manner. I wondered what he was doing; then I saw he was holding on to an erection. I was in a dazed state and it felt weird as I wondered what he was doing. Then I saw a yellow box of condoms in his right hand. I came to my senses and rebuked him. The spirit turned around and ran out of the bedroom. I had been through hell for the chance to be with the Lord's daughter, but I had no desire to settle for anyone's son. The devil was literally trying to change my sexual preference, as a way of turning me away from any of the Lord's daughter's. I highly encourage people to pray for their current and future spouses. The devil is adamant about preventing or destroying God-ordained relationships.

I also dreamt I was in a wrestling coach's office. He was a short stocky man who obviously had a wrestler's strength. The coach was speaking to me when the Holy Spirit said the coach was going to rape me. My initial reaction was to size up the situation to see how I would defend myself when he attacked. One thing to my advantage was the desk between us. His door was open so I decided to do the best thing by walking out of the office. The devil masquerading as the wrestling coach tried to get me back into his office but I refused. I do not always receive such clear warnings from the Lord, but when I do, I need to take heed. I learned my lesson from when I mishandled the warning from the Lord in 2015. You will never go wrong by obeying the Lord.

The final sample dream was the most horrifying. The dream started with me and other "people", whose faces I could not see, in the kitchen of a Christian couple I watch on YouTube. The story was I had eaten another guest's chicken from their refrigerator, even though I never ate anything in the dream. However, when you are in a demonic dream, it does not matter what you did or did not do... Anyhow, the dream continued with me trying to leave the house, but none of the doors led out of the house. [*Demonic sometimes provide no way of escape. It seemed as if every door led to either the kitchen or the bedroom. A dream in a kitchen oftentimes speaks of a place of preparation while a bedroom represents a place of making and renewing covenant.*] The "man" had changed into pajamas but with shoes for outdoors. I noticed I was getting weak. I felt drugged. I was rapidly losing consciousness as I became more aware of the pounding sound of my heart. I was also painfully aware of what was going to happen if I could not regain my strength and consciousness. The spirit masquerading as the man's wife "graciously" opened a door that led outside and told me to run. However, "she" was starting the game instead of giving me a way of escape. I was getting a few minutes head start before "her husband" would hunt me down and rape me. My strength and level of consciousness were fading, fast. It would have been counterproductive to make a quick break. Rapid movement would have increased the drug's circulation throughout my system. I decided it was best to stumble up a nearby hill and hide in some bushes, hoping the spirit would think I had ran into the woods. In addition, I walked by an area with gravel prior to going up the hill. With the little strength I had left, I grabbed a rock, big enough to potentially kill the "man" who was coming after me. I slowly blacked out, with my heart beating harder but slower, while holding on to the rock. The rock was symbolic of holding on to the Lord. Even in a demonic dream, where it seemed as if I was doomed, the

Lord showed Himself mighty, my Rock and Saving Grace. So, like Moses said, *'Because I will publish the name of the Lord: ascribe ye greatness unto **our God**. **He is the Rock**, His work is perfect: for all His ways are judgment: a God of truth and without iniquity, just and right is He.'* ~ Deuteronomy 32:3-4

The last dream exemplifies why eating in a demonically induced dream is an awful thing. Also, demonic dreams often leave a person feeling fearful and/or hopeless. It is a hopeless feeling trying to escape but finding no way out. But even more hopeless are the dreams I have had where calling upon Jesus had no effect. One such example was a dream where a demon that looked like a dark plume of smoke that reached the ceiling started coming towards me. I rebuked it twice in the name of Jesus, but it kept advancing and eventually began going down my throat. I started pulling it out of my mouth until it got to the point where if I pulled it out I would have ripped out my tongue and bled to death. I so missed the days when sleep meant rest instead of life threatening spiritual warfare. I desperately wanted the Lord to make these attacks stop.

Sexual Assaults

I experienced at least one sexual assault per month, for almost five years. One of the lowest points during this process was when I begged the Lord to kill me than to have me endure another sexual assault. I was done with sexual immorality in my life so I did not want it in my dreams, especially with defiling demons. I was livid when I was assaulted again, then I stopped counting after the fourth sexual assault, after I had asked the Lord to kill me instead. Some people enjoy having sexual encounters with demons, oftentimes out of ignorance of the devil's devices. I vowed to the Lord that I would not kiss another woman until my wedding day. Based on that vow, whenever I dreamt of a woman wanting to kiss me or kissing me, it was a devil trying to be my unlawfully wedded spouse. Likewise, there were times when I had dreams of being seduced and other times I would start having a dream where I was in the midst of a sex act. I thought these attacks would end if I could simply rebuke the devil in a dream. However, I dreamt of a spirit masquerading as a woman, masturbating in an attempt to entice me into sexual sin. But I walked over to the spirit and kept repeating in its ear, *"The Lord rebuke you, the Lord rebuke you, the Lord rebuke you..."* That victory was short lived, which made me wonder what in the world I needed to do for these attacks to end. I may have hated God at times during this process, but I certainly hated life. There were times when I did not want to say anything to the Lord and I did not want Him to say anything to me. Those moods were short-lived. I hated the devil, but my attitude was if God did not love me enough to stop these attacks, I was still going to love Him, even if He hated me. Yet, one of the benefits to these attacks was to teach me to never leave the Lord's daughter uncovered and unprotected. I also learned the meaning of unconditional love.

I no longer instantly doubt when a person says, "The devil made me do it." I dreamt I was like an FBI agent on a stakeout with two other agents, a husband and wife. I was surprised when I looked behind me and saw what they were making. Then suddenly, my spirit was pushed into the man's body, which resulted in me having sex, at least briefly, with the spirit masquerading as his wife. Dreaming of lusting after or having sex with another person spouse is potentially a covenant with a spirit spouse that has multiple human "spouses", a spirit of adultery (from which I had been delivered), and a spirit of death. You may be wondering how committing adultery (in a dream) could represent a covenant with death. This is so because Proverbs 6:32 says: "But whoso committeth adultery with a woman lacketh understanding: he that doeth it destroyeth his own soul." In addition, Leviticus 20, the 10th verse states, "And the man that committeth adultery with another man's wife, even he that committeth adultery with his neighbour's wife, the adulterer and the adulteress shall surely be put to death." It is worthy to note that Jesus let the adulteress go in part because of to the Pharisees hypocritical application and violation of the above Law (John 8:1-11). The Pharisees did not bring the man to stand judgment with the woman. Likewise, the Lord sees how the devil is trying to lead me into sin, and then accuse me of being a sinner in an effort to illegally gain legal access to my life. If you are avoiding sin, the Lord sees what the devil is trying to do to you too and the Lord is a righteous judge. The events in the dream made me wonder what the Great Tribulation will be like especially because the devil knows his days are truly numbered.

I had a few hundred sexual encounters in dreams and visions during a four-year period. To my chagrin, I felt like a young girl whose mother's partner had been visiting her at night. But when the daughter cried out to her mother, instead of swiftly taking the appropriate actions to end it, the "mother" allows the attacks to continue. The things I have endured taught me that **the Lord has two unenviable perspectives. The Lord gets to see the ugliness of His children willingly engaging in sin followed by them suffering the consequences of those sins**.

If people check my church attendance record to see if I love the Lord they will make the wrong assessment. A study of Lazarus's death reveals why Jesus did not immediately respond to Lazarus's family's request to save his life. Even though Jesus allowed Lazarus to die, knowing He would resurrect him, Jesus still wept (John 11). Some people's testimonies tell of how Jesus showed up at the perfect time for them. But, how about those testimonies where the Lord showed up after their hopes and dreams were dashed or even dead? Will you still love the Lord and be excited to see Him when His perfect timing is (seemingly) too late for you? Will you still love the Lord if you feel like He failed you? The enemy was pushing me to curse God and die because of His apparent failure to stick to His Word by contending with those who were contending with me (Isaiah 49:25). The devil was trying to convince me to walk away from the Lord in grand style, to include calling the Lord a liar as I burn the Bible. A part of why the Lord wanted me to write this book during the trial was so I could still harness the rawness of the emotions I dealt with. I say things with candor because I am a communicator and no trial is easy. Too many people have given sanitized testimonies which makes them seem weak for grimacing and complaining during their trial while that person seemingly endured without ever complaining. We should not be hypocrites when we share our testimonies. I know I had undoubtedly been involved in sexual immorality throughout the years that was worthy of being cast into hell. Yet, a major part of my frustration was finally being committed to my vow to remain celibate, and every act with a devil was defiling, to my destiny and my soul.

The most significant marker for me that the trial is over would be the end of the monthly sexual assaults, especially the dreams where I would wake up in the midst of being sexually assaulted, or having been sexually assaulted without realizing it, until a bit later. I publicly proclaimed I would not marry a devil, a daughter of the devil, or even one of the Lord's daughter's that He had not ordained for me. I do not like being disrespected especially when I made a commitment to the Lord that another entity was violating. In fact, a part of the enemy's sinister plan was to lead me into physical sexual sin. In real life, the devil was unsuccessful in leading me into sexual immorality so he resorted to dreams and visions. I fast in part to crucify my flesh, even to the point where I went shopping for groceries towards the end of a 10-day water only fast. I would not succumb to the temptation of any food. I had the incentive of wanting freedom more than food. In fact, when the Lord directed me to do that fast, I thought it was to break the hold of the spirit trying to be my wife. Sadly, I went through a situation where a seducing spirit, masquerading as the Holy Spirit, tried to convince me to marry someone else. It was similar to how the devil approached Jesus after He had been fasting after 40 days and 40 nights. The devil has a knack for trying to exploit our weakness or when we are in a weakened state. By the way, to my chagrin, I later found out that someone had been praying for me to get into a relationship with the other person.

I went through these things, which caused me to reflect on my sinful past. I know Jesus paid the price to redeem me from my sins and cleanse me from all unrighteousness, but if these sufferings were in anyway related to my past, I do not ever want sin in my presence ever again. It also gives me a zeal to warn people about the consequences of sin. I do not wish my experiences on anyone because it is as close to hell as I ever want anyone to be. Yet, despite what you have read, I suffered worse atrocities, some of which I never want to share.

Witchcrafts

When the newly anointed king Jehu stormed towards Jezreel to begin tearing down the remnant of king Ahab's regime, he had the following encounter with the deceased king's son, Joram:

"And Joram said, *'Make ready.'*

And his chariot was made ready. And Joram king of Israel and Ahaziah king of Judah went out, each in his chariot, and they went out against Jehu, and met him in the portion of Naboth the Jezreelite. And it came to pass, when Joram saw Jehu, that he said, *'Is it peace, Jehu?'*

And he answered, *'What peace, so long as the whoredoms of thy mother Jezebel and her witchcrafts are so many?'*

And Joram turned his hands, and fled, and said to Ahaziah, *'There is treachery, O Ahaziah.'*

And Jehu drew a bow with his full strength, and smote Jehoram between his arms, and the arrow went out at his heart, and he sunk down in his chariot." ~ 2 Kings 9:21-26

One of the goals of witchcraft is to rob us of our peace. Jesus is the Prince of Peace, and witchcraft is aimed at diminishing or even destroying our relationship with Christ Jesus.

I had numerous subtle dreams, visions and other encounters indicating witchcraft activities in my life. Conversely, some encounters were blatantly vicious. I was in for a surprise when I was putting an anti-weed liner in my front yard before adding some mulch. My metal rake unearthed a straw object, one that looked like parts of a broom. I had never seen a voodoo doll in real life until, that day. I pray all of the enemy's works will go up in flames like the doll I set it on fire. I also had a vision of a demonic altar that a witch had raised up against me. Obviously, such a thing is idolatry, a violation of the Lord's first Commandment where He said, *'Thou shalt have no other gods before Me.'* ~ Exodus 20:3. It is idolatrous to set up an altar to another god. In addition, even though it is set up to hurt or destroy a person, it is also idolatrous to set up an altar to focus on another person. I even had a dream of a pentagram drawn in chalk on the left side of my driveway. In addition, I saw several of my shoes on the lines of the pentagram. So, while I was focusing on the Lord, evil people, workers of iniquity, were focused on me.

We oftentimes see ourselves where we are while the enemy sees and attacks who we can be, and if it were not for God's glory, the enemy would succeed. It is important to discern when the Lord has great things in store for us (Jeremiah 29:11). That is why the enemy dedicates time, effort, and other precious resources to try to stop us from fulfilling our Godly calling. We typically see ourselves on levels below where we are. The enemy may not know what the Lord has in store for us, but he is excellent at spotting our potential, and then try to kill it. A similar situation existed when a royal decree was issued around the time of Moses' and later Jesus' birth to kill baby boys less than two years old. This was not because those infants were a threat. On the contrary, it was because of one of them was going to grow up and destroy the enemy's kingdom. Moses' birth came at a time when the

Lord's promise to Abraham indicated that his offspring 400 years captivity was coming to its fullness. Below is the Word of the Lord to Abraham regarding this matter, notice the special emphasis on how the Lord would afflict those who afflicted His children. Similarly, the Lord will make the enemy pay for messing with you:

> *'Know of a surety that thy seed shall be a stranger in a land that is not theirs, and shall serve them; and they shall afflict them four hundred years; And also that nation, whom they shall serve, will I judge: and afterward shall they come out with great substance.'* ~ Genesis 15:13-14

Signs that the Messiah had come were clearly evident when Jesus was born. For example, the wise men came from the east and king Herod had the chief priests and scribes verify their revelation about the Messiah's birth by searching the Scriptures (Matthew 2). The devil had a vested interest to kill the baby boys who had the potential to destroy his kingdom. It was a tremendous defeat to the devil for even one person to get delivered. Moses led 600,000 men out of captivity (Exodus 12:37). When you add the unnumbered women and children, more than likely, at least a million people had escaped from the devil's grasp. Moses had quite the deliverance ministry, and that deliverance was in deed a process. Those people were delivered from Egypt, delivered from the Egyptians by the Red Sea, delivered from the Egyptian mindset in the wilderness (where the older generations were purged), and then delivered into the Promise Land. Consequently, deliverance is not complete until the Lord delivers us from where we were and puts us where He wants us to be.

The greatest deliverance ministry and minister, greater than Moses and John the Baptist, combined, is Jesus the Christ. He had been delivering people since the beginning of time. How could that be we may wonder? Well, Jesus is the Lamb who was slain from the foundation of the earth, to redeem us from the curse of sin and death. Jesus also permanently translated us from the kingdom of darkness to the kingdom of Light. The devil hates deliverers. So when the Lord establishes a deliverer, it will not go well for the unrepentant captors, and the witchcraft practitioners (Ezekiel 13:17-23, Jeremiah 5:26-31). We began this discussion with Jehu saying there would be no peace as long as Jezebel and her witchcrafts are so many, let us look at how things ended for Jezebel and her witchcrafts:

> "And when Jehu was come to Jezreel, Jezebel heard of it; and she painted her face, and tired her head, and looked out at a window. And as Jehu entered in at the gate, she said, *'Had Zimri peace, who slew his master?'*
>
> And he lifted up his face to the window, and said, *'Who is on my side? Who?'*
>
> And there looked out to him two or three eunuchs.
>
> And he said, *'Throw her down.'*
>
> So they threw her down: and some of her blood was sprinkled on the wall, and on the horses: and he trode her under foot.
>
> And when he was come in, he did eat and drink, and said, *'Go, see now this cursed woman, and bury her: for she is a king's daughter.'*
>
> And they went to bury her: but they found no more of her than the skull, and the feet, and the palms of her hands.
>
> Wherefore they came again, and told him. And he said, *'This is the Word of the Lord, which he spake by His servant Elijah the Tishbite, saying, 'In the portion of Jezreel shall dogs eat the flesh of Jezebel: And the carcase of Jezebel shall be as dung upon the face of the field in the portion of Jezreel; so that they shall not say, 'This is Jezebel.'"* ~ 2 Kings 9:30-37

Jezebel's death was not the end for her. No, I am not referring to the "jezebel spirit". This is about her suffering in hell and later the lake of fire, which is where unrepentant witches will go. Every evil deed they have done will come back unto them, like a boomerang. Therefore, "Be not deceived; God is not mocked: for whatsoever a man soweth, that shall he also reap. For he that soweth to his flesh shall of the flesh reap corruption; but he that soweth to the Spirit shall of the Spirit reap life everlasting." ~ Galatians 6:7 8

In closing this section about witchcraft, Jehu did not fall for Jezebel's attempt to seduce him or to engage him in conversation. Jehu simply had her thrown down. Likewise, we need to immediately cast down every evil work sent against us. We should not tolerate Jezebel and her witchcrafts

(Revelation 2:18-23). Even though we cannot throw down witches anymore, we can throw down witchcraft by not becoming involved in any type of witchcraft as stated in the following scripture:

> For though we walk in the flesh, we do not war after the flesh: (For the weapons of our warfare are not carnal, but mighty through God to the pulling down of strong holds;) Casting down imaginations, and every high thing that exalteth itself against the knowledge of God, and bringing into captivity every thought to the obedience of Christ; And having in a readiness to revenge all disobedience, when your obedience is fulfilled." ~ 2 Corinthians 10:3-6

The Marine Kingdom

I thought it was absolutely ridiculous when I initially heard about demons called "water spirits" from the devil's "marine kingdom", especially since most humans live on land. However, things had drastically changed when I saw a video about a year later with a minister mocking another minister for speaking about the marine kingdom. A major shift for me was as a result of the Lord letting me know I was in a battle with devils from the marine kingdom. The Bible does not spell out everything clearly, especially when it comes to satan, which is a part of why I was inspired to write this book. Some people will relate to the things I am sharing while others will think it is utter nonsense. With respect to the former, it is because they have had these experiences but did not know where to turn. They may have reached out for help, but no one believed so they resigned to suffer silence. In fact, earlier today, I shared some of my experiences and the person asked if I was suffering from Post Traumatic Stress Disorder. The answer was a resounding no; I have not had issues since returning from the Middle East. People who have come under intense spiritual warfare would have never asked that question, yet I was not offended by it. I know everyone does not and will not understand what I have been going through. On the contrary, meeting someone with shared and seemingly unbelievable experiences is like finding an oasis in a desert. I have certainly learned to not doubt a person's experiences based on my lack of knowledge or personal experience. The enemy loves to operate in the shadows, which is one of the reasons why he hates me for exposing his operations. However, after everything he has done to me, it is the least I can do in return.

One of the ways I knew a spirit from the marine kingdom was working against me was because of dreams or visions with activities in water. There were times when I woke up from dreams wondering why I had stood in a puddle of water, which seemed out of place. Or, why I dreamt of dirty water flooding my house, starting upstairs. I ignorantly got up and checked to see if I had a leaky roof. Other dreams involved being in a river back in Jamaica, or in a sea or ocean. Some dreams were downright sinister where the devil did not even bother masking the evil. In one dream, I looked at the sky and saw a beautiful crimson red sunset. However, upon closer examination, I saw a devil in the clouds. I started backing away from the water's edge but got pushed in. Another dream involved "me" stepping into a river, one that was usually crystal clear was murky and much deeper than in real life. I needed to breathe but I could not because I knew I would either drown or ingest an evil (water) spirit. I concluded that the enemy was trying to force me to invite him into my life. In another dream, rocks created a pool in the sea, about 50 meters away from the shore. I was in the swells of the pool, which seemed normal, but the water started swirling around, with me in it, like the spin cycle of a washing machine or a brew in a cauldron. It started tossing me to and fro, exposing me to the dangerous rocks. Several other dreams involved water coming over my head. I realized that the cunning enemy was even masquerading as family members who were drowning to get me into the water. One of the most sinister dreams involved a spirit tackling me as if we were playing football or rugby. The next thing I knew, bubbles surrounded us as we rapidly descended to depths of the sea, against my will. I would not have been able to escape and make it back to the surface alive without supplemental oxygen.

A deliverance minister had gotten frustrated with me because she said something was going on that the Lord was not telling her. She recommended that I spend some time with God to see if I am really saved because no devil should be able to do the things the devil has been doing to me. She also said the Jesus she served was not as weak as mine. Mind you, we were serving the same Jesus. In addition, during the first deliverance session, they led me through the prayer of salvation (again), just to be on the safe side. In addition, the ministers cast the devils out of me in (their) Jesus' name. That could have been the most devastating event during the tribulation period. It made me feel like Job when his friends accused him of unrighteousness and being the source of why the devil had afflicted him. I thank the Lord for not remaining silent during the test. He did something that night to prevent what the deliverance minister said from wrecking me. Prior to calling in, I saw another minister's social media page where he said some people will not understand your "Bethlehem road experience". The message was about the long and painful journey Naomi had taken. Her journey was so emotionally taxing, that when she returned from Moab with Ruth, people were excited to see her and called her Naomi. To which she responded, *'Call me not Naomi, call me Mara: for the Almighty hath dealt very bitterly with me. I went out full and the Lord hath brought me home again empty: why then call ye me Naomi, seeing the Lord hath testified against me, and the Almighty hath afflicted me?'* ~ Ruth 2:20-21

I do not take it lightly when I hear people making a mockery of things they have not experienced or understand. It is an absolutely horrible thing to hear anyone making a mockery of something someone else is struggling with. I was at a meeting where a minister spoke of falling asleep as soon as his head hits the pillow, and not waking up until the alarm goes off. Well, I can attest that some people are avoiding sleep because they know of the hell that awaits them. In addition, the spiritual warfare serves as their alarm clock. There were times when I would have preferred going to a seminary, and had some sleepless nights studying, instead of enduring relentless spiritual attacks.

Bed Sandwich

Of the thousands of demonic dreams and visions I have had, arguably, one of the worst took place in a darkened room. Things from the kingdom of darkness frequently occur in darkness or a pseudo light. In this case, I was fearfully lying in a bed sandwiched between the mattress and the box spring. [Note: *The enemy was trying to illegally gain legal access into my life by claiming I was sinning against God. Despite numerous demonic visitations, I never ran or hid from the enemy. But the enemy was trying to induce fear, a violation of the Word of God, which says, "For God hath not given us the spirit of fear; but of power, and of love, and of a sound mind." ~ 2 Timothy 1:7*] I was in that position to hopefully avoid a powerful evil presence that was coming into the bedroom. The devil entered the room and "I" hoped it would pass by. It was on the left side while I was tucked away on the right, then it came over to my side. It lifted the mattress without touching it. The devil looked like a dark shadow in a dark room. It stretched out its hands towards me and I saw the power projecting out of the hands, like the afterburners on a fighter jet's engines on full thrust. The stream of energy started at my feet, pushing them to the centerline of the bed. I woke up as the devil was projecting a power into my legs and working his way up to my hips that was driving me to the middle of the bed. I woke up feeling as if my body had been displaced, as if the experience was not simply a dream.

I woke up in shock wondering what in the world had just happened. It was early in the morning, but I immediately reached out to some "prayer warriors" for intercessory prayer support. I even reached out to other intercessors a few hours after waking up. Sadly, no one ever reported receiving any information from the Lord regarding what had happened in the dream. **No one spoke of the opposition I was up against.** If this was the enemy's attempt to force me to marry that witch, or any of his daughters, it was not going to work. I had already been down that road in 2015, when I did not realize people were using witchcraft against me in an effort to force me to marry the witch. I also thought about how people were going to hell for this, and the other attacks, IF they do not repent. The devil was also going to find out that my no meant no.

It is truly purely by God's grace why I have been surviving. Many people would not be able to sleep if they had a demon in their house, and especially one that was refusing to leave. In the last 10 months, I have never felt at peace for more than 3 days. The attacks have been relentless, especially when I tried to sleep. Do not let me ever hear you pray and ask the Lord to not let someone rest until you get your way. After what I have experienced, there is no telling how I will react to that form of witchcraft.

Morgellons

Some people are in mental institutions because of spiritual problems and demonic afflictions. One of the worst experiences the Lord allowed me to suffer is what is known as "Morgellons Disease". Despite potential physically apparent manifestations, such as sores, which I did not have, its signs and symptoms are considered psychosomatic. It simply does not make sense for a person to complain of bugs crawling under his or her skin but no medical device can detect them. Baffled, therefore it makes sense to the medical community to rationalize that the "bugs" are contrived. After all, the most plausible explanation, which is spiritual, is not usually plausible to them at all.

For persons who have never experienced Morgellons, it is not something to wish upon your worst enemy. I was trying to sleep one night and I had a strange sensation in that troublesome spot in the lower left quadrant of my abdomen. It felt like someone had placed a bag of cockroaches in my side, broke it open, and I had cockroaches crawling all over my body and under my skin. For those who have experienced this, you are not crazy, especially if you had a dream where someone injected something into you or you were eating. For some people, numerous bugs crawling on top of their skin would be horrible enough. But, at least under those conditions, the person could easily get the bugs off. Sadly, that is not quite the case if those "bugs" are under your skin. The sensation may cause a person to scratch and break his or her skin open to let the bugs out. There were times when I hit my body to kill the sensation. Unfortunately, scratching one's skin may cause infections and hitting may cause bruising. We know devils are wicked but how wicked must someone be to project such a thing on another person?

I have heard people testify of the torments that they saw witches suffering from in hell. Now I have a better idea of why they suffer immensely in hell, and deservingly so. God is not mocked, and we will reap what we have sown (Galatians 6:7-8). It may seem as if the wicked are prospering without suffering the consequences of their actions here on earth, but eventually, they will reap it in hell if they do not repent. There are many people in hell, begging for one more chance to repent but they will not get it. The Lord's judgment is final. It is very significant when the Lord repeats Himself. Jesus described hell as a place of torments and He repeated the following three times: *'Where their worm dieth not, and the fire is not quenched.'* ~ Mark 9:44, 46, 48

Based on this tribulation, I am in alignment with the Lord's will. He does not want anyone to go to hell. His desire is for everyone to repent of their sins and claim and faithfully serve Christ Jesus as their Lord and Savior. This tribulation is as far away from the Lord and as close to hell as I ever want to be. I cannot imagine how horrible hell truly is, and I knew the Lord was going to get me through this, but there is no escaping hell, the horrors, the hunger, the thirst, the sleep deprivation, sounds, sights, smells... One of the most disconcerting things about hell is calling on Christ and knowing that He will never come. Crying out to the devil will not work either because he will be busy trying to deal with his own problems (torments).

There were times when I asked the Lord for a break so I could get a little bit of sleep, and He graciously obliged. There are no tangible breaks in hell: the torments are persistent and they last forever. Jesus said the lake of fire was created for the devil and his (fallen) angels (Matthew 25:41). I pray that workers of iniquity come across this book and repent. I thankfully received deliverance after the first major episode of battling this disease, which is actually a demonic manifestation. If anyone has "Morgellons Disease", they should seek the Lord for deliverance. The afflicted person is not crazy. On the contrary, devils are tormenting them in an attempt to make them go crazy. Deliverance is the children's bread and the Lord's children are starving.

Thorn In The Flesh

There were times when my side felt normal, but I would have an encounter where someone or something was either on or touched my left side. Then, shortly after waking up, I felt the manifestation on my left side again. It was odd how it kept happening on my left side. But then again, a bride stands on the left side of a groom during their wedding ceremony.

In an encounter, I dreamt I was lying on my back with someone on my left side. I looked down and saw a woman clinging to me, like a barnacle on a ship's hull. I realized it was a short woman, hugging me tightly with her face buried in my side. I recognized the witch and woke up as I was about to pry her off from me. If someone invades your dream and hide his or her face, it clearly shows the person knows he or she is trespassing. In this case, the witch was trying to hold on to someone else's man. She also knew I did not want her, but was still trying to be in my life, like someone claiming squatter's rights. Spiritual actions such as these are that of a thief. It reminds me of one night when I was driving behind a truck and the Lord highlighted the numbers "101" on the license plate. I searched the Bible and the Lord showed me the answer in John 10:1, when Jesus said, *Verily,*

verily, I say unto you, He that entereth not by the door into the sheepfold, but climbeth up some other way, the same is a thief and a robber.' Shortly afterwards, the witch tried coming into my life, by *'some other way'*. Again, thank the Lord for not being totally silent during the test, for everything He has delivered me from thus far, and especially for where He is leading me to.

CHAPTER 4

UNIVERSITY OF ADVERSITY

*And I heard a loud voice saying in heaven, 'Now is come salvation, and strength, and the kingdom of our God, and the power of His Christ: for the accuser of our brethren is cast down, which accused them before our God day and night. **And they overcame him by the blood of the Lamb, and by the word of their testimony; and they loved not their lives unto the death.** Therefore rejoice, ye heavens, and ye that dwell in them. Woe to the inhabiters of the earth and of the sea! For the devil is come down unto you, having great wrath, because he knoweth that he hath but a short time.'* ~ Revelation 12:10-12

Holy Spirit-Led Deliverance

Deliverance is a result of a divine confrontation between Christ or His angels and the kingdom of darkness. I was desperate to receive deliverance, and I did everything I was told to do to gain freedom. I spent a year fasting and praying, and, I anointed my property line and house, including my doorways, windows, mirrors, pipelines, and other areas. I even anointed myself. I did multiple all-night prayer vigils, but the things that ministers with international deliverance ministries successfully used for others did not work for me. It taught me humility and demonstrated that deliverance is not a formula. Whatever the Lord has in store for me to do for His glory, I am simply His vessel. Nothing will happen because of me so I have to become even more humble in order to remain under the Holy Spirit's lordship. After all, "For as many as are led by the Spirit of God, they are the sons of God. For ye have not received the spirit of bondage again to fear; but ye have received the Spirit of adoption, whereby we cry, *'Abba, Father.'*" ~ Romans 8:14-15

Every minister and ministry needs to submit to the lordship of the Holy Spirit because He continuously points and leads us to Christ Jesus. **A minister cannot rely on previously effective methods to obtain future success.** Take note of Jesus healing blind eyes and how it varied. The Lord may vary things to demonstrate His creativity because He is the Creator. He may also vary things to overcome the enemy's strongholds and evolving strategies. God's ways are not always our way and neither are His thoughts our thoughts. We need to align our ways and thoughts with His through the Holy Spirit. Being a Christian, and especially a minister of Christ Jesus, requires having a close relationship with the Lord. Effective communication is vital in every relationship, and especially our relationship with the Lord.

Humility

God resists the proud but gives grace to the humble (James 4:6, 1 Peter 5:5). The Lord also humbles before He exalts. Great examples of the Lord's humbling process are Joseph's 13 years in captivity before becoming Egypt's governor, David spending years on the run to escape Saul's life-threatening pursuits, and Moses spending 40 years shepherding flock. Moses's process resulted in him becoming the humblest man on the face of the earth (Numbers 12:3). As a result, the Lord entrusted him with leading a nation. My very painful experience has humbled me but I am still a work in progress. In 2013, a chaplain said I reminded him of David. I had no idea how profound those words were. Things became evident when I got persecuted like David, but mostly in the spiritual realm. I had the chance to kill one of my persecutors, but I left vengeance up to the Lord's. One of the major differences between combat in Afghanistan and Iraq were the Rules of Engagement (ROE). The ROE were more restrictive in Afghanistan and was like fighting with only one hand. Similarly, in my situation, the Lord established a ROE and there were lines I could not cross regardless of what the enemy did.

There is a military combat specialty called Psychological Operations

(PSYOP). The poltergeist in my house was like a PSYOPs agent. Its assignment included trying to cause me to overreact by cursing the humans working against me or taking drastic physical countermeasures. There are times when the enemy will provoke a victim to wrath to make him or her look like the predator. However, based on experiences I have had after committing personal transgressions, I trusted the Lord to handle things. I knew it was best to patiently wait upon the Lord while enduring the afflictions knowing that in the fullness of time the Lord would repay the enemy. My mission was to focus on Jesus and trust Him with rendering justice in due time (Colossians 3:2).

God's Gifts and Calling

The Holy Spirit gives one or all nine of His spiritual gifts to people, in accordance with His will (1 Corinthians 12:1-12). Some people have a gift or gifts from the Holy Spirit but they lack the fruit of the Holy Spirit (Galatians 5:22-23). We must exercise great care with respect to the gifts of the Holy Spirit, and this includes using them to serve and glorify Jesus instead of ourselves, which ultimately glorifies the devil. People do not always set out to misuse their gifts. Such actions are oftentimes the product of rejection or abuse, from within the family and/or church. It is best to use the gifts of the Holy Spirit in accordance with the Lord's way, will, and Word, and His timing. Many people are in trouble with the Lord without realizing it, partially because their spiritual gifts are still functional, and possibly quite profitable. The commensurate fruit of the Holy Spirit are essential as Jesus emphasized in one of His scariest declarations:

> *'Not every one that saith unto Me, 'Lord, Lord', shall enter into the kingdom of heaven; but he that doeth the will of My Father which is in heaven. Many will say to Me in that day, 'Lord, Lord, have we not prophesied in Thy name? And in Thy name have cast out devils? And in Thy name done many wonderful works?' And then will I profess unto them, I never knew you: depart from Me, ye that work iniquity.'* ~ Matthew 7:21-23

Saul continued serving as king for years after Samuel the seer told him the Lord had rejected him as king (1 Samuel 13:13-14, 15:22-23). Then the Lord sent the prophet to anoint David to replace Saul as king over Israel (1 Samuel 16). Many people quote Romans 11:29 by saying, "For the gifts and calling of God are without repentance", without realizing it is a double-edged sword. If the gifts of the Lord stopped working, it would serve as a major sign that maybe a person's relationship with the Lord is in disrepair. Subtle signs of a strained relationship include not being used as mightily or frequently as in times past. Saul did not feel the magnitude of his strained relationship with the Lord until shortly before his death (1 Samuel 28). Another of the many lessons I learned during this process was to discern when I was operating within the Lord's will. The enemy tried to subtly mislead me on numerous occasions, but I knew that following his promptings would have taken me outside of the Lord's will.

Another source of error is assuming that the gifts and calling from the Lord are for personal use. The Lord demonstrated the importance of serving others, especially when He was on the cross, and also when He said: *'Neither be ye called masters: for one is your Master, even Christ.* **But he that is greatest among you shall be your servant.** *And whosoever shall exalt himself shall be abased; and he that shall humble himself shall be exalted.'* ~ Matthew 23:10-12. The Lord will make a process very painful to ensure His servant is a humble and submitted vessel.

Prophets have gone astray, and even succumbed to pride, because they believed they could prophesy at will. That includes by grossly misinterpreting and misapplying the Scriptures as stated in 1 Corinthians 14:32: "...the spirits of the prophets are subject to the prophets." Another Scriptural guardrail to keep prophets on the straight and narrow path is 2 Peter 1:21, which states, "...prophecy came not in old time by the will of man: but holy men of God spake as they were moved by the Holy Ghost." The Lord also gave other admonishments regarding receiving a message from Him and waiting for His permission to release it. Some people are doing exactly what the Lord warned us not to do, which is to prophesy from their own soul (mind, will, and emotions): This is exemplified in Jeremiah 14:14:

> "Then the Lord said unto me, *'The prophets prophesy lies in My name: I sent them not, neither have I commanded them, neither spake unto them: they prophesy unto you a false vision and divination, and a thing of nought, and the deceit of their heart.'"*

I also learned that there is less leeway for error when prophesying in comparison to casting out devils. If a person gives a false prophecy, which may make the person an errant prophet instead of a false one, that person can get labeled as a false prophet. However, being a false prophet is more of what I would describe as a heart condition. For example, the prophet from Bethel who did not fear God as evidenced by knowingly telling a lie in His name (1 Kings 13:11-32). False prophets will also do everything to escape accountability for missing the mark, except admit their error and simply repent. It is a very bad thing, a very poor track record, if a prophet gets 9 out of 10 (predictive) prophecies wrong. On the other hand, if a deliverance minister only casts out 1 of 10 devils, that is very good. In some cases, the minister may identify multiple devils but not cast all of them out. Or, the minister may even try to cast a devil out and fail without being considered a failure. I did not choose the process I endured or the type of ministry the Lord has called me to, but like all ministers, I know I am most effective when I am doing the Lord's will. This includes doing what He has called and instructed me to do.

Christ Jesus is our model for all things. Even though He was God in the flesh, He was effective because of His submission to the Heavenly Father's will. We know "…there are three that bear record in heaven, the Father, the Word [Jesus], and the Holy Ghost: and these three are one." ~ 1 John 5:7. All three function as one, which is how we need to model our respective ministries with the Holy Spirit as our guide. Jesus gave us the key to His effectiveness as follows:

> "Then answered Jesus and said unto them, *'Verily, verily, I say unto you,* ***The Son can do nothing of Himself, but what He seeth the Father do: for what things soever He doeth, these also doeth the Son likewise.*** *For the Father loveth the Son, and sheweth Him all things that Himself doeth: and He will shew Him greater works than these, that ye may marvel. For as the Father raiseth up the dead, and quickeneth them; even so the Son quickeneth whom He will. For the Father judgeth no man, but hath committed all judgment unto the Son: That all men should honour the Son, even as they honour the Father. He that honoureth not the Son honoureth not the Father which hath sent Him. Verily, verily, I say unto you, He that heareth My Word, and believeth on Him that sent Me, hath everlasting life, and shall not come into condemnation; but is passed from death unto life."* ~ John 5:19-24

Jesus, the Son of God, did what He saw His Father in heaven doing, which brought honor to the Father. So, even though Jesus was and is worthy of honor, He did things to honor the One who sent Him. Likewise, the Holy Spirit is worthy of honor. Many people seemingly forget that the Holy Spirit is God's spiritual power. Moreover, like Christ Jesus, the Holy Spirit does not minister to bring glory to Himself:

> *'Howbeit when He, the Spirit of Truth, is come, He will guide you into all truth: for He shall not speak of Himself; but whatsoever He shall hear, that shall He speak: and He will shew you things to come. He shall glorify Me: for He shall receive of Mine, and shall shew it unto you.'* ~ John 16:13-14

The Holy Spirit points us to Christ Jesus who in turn points and leads us to the Father. **Amazing things happen when we look at our gifts and calling as being from God for His glory.** We are simply vessels whom He chooses to use at various times for a variety of purposes. Be careful of any minister who draws you to him or her but does little to no work to point you to Christ Jesus. Paul said, *'Be ye followers of me, even as I also am of Christ.'* ~ 1 Corinthians 11:1. Do not follow anyone who is not ultimately leading you to having a deeper personal relationship with Christ. When we look at the example of Elijah, he called down fire on Mount Carmel to lead the people back to the Lord, which was a part of why the Lord entrusted him with that ability. **The process prepares a person to responsibly steward the gifts and calling of the Lord.** Elijah had that ability, and other gifts, but his ministry was about leading people to the Lord. Hence, while on Mount Carmel opposing the 450 false prophets, "…Elijah came unto all the people, and said, *'How long halt ye between two opinions? If the Lord be God, follow Him: but if baal, then follow him.'* And the people answered him not a word." ~ 1 Kings 18:21. If a minister says it is dangerous to have a personal relationship with the Lord, run away from that minister and ministry. As ministers, we are to help lead others to a higher level of spiritual maturity by developing a deeper relationship with the Lord. Jesus said His sheep know His voice and another they will not follow. A key lesson learned while seeking deliverance was to seek the Lord first. I could go to the most gifted minister and still not receive deliverance if it was not in accordance with the Lord's timing. What Jesus said also applies to deliverance: *'But seek ye first the kingdom of God, and His righteousness; and all these things shall be added unto you.'* ~ Matthew 6:33

Another reminder that the gifts and calling are the Lord's is a person can have gifts and a calling but they are only effective if the Lord is using them. The prophet from Bethel in 1 Kings 13 serves as an excellent example in this area too. He lived in Bethel but the Lord sent a prophet from Judah to prophesy in Bethel instead. The clear instructions I received from the Lord to defeat the devils was to do a series of fasts, but He did not specify how long. I wanted to finish the battle quickly so I went on an aggressive 30-day fast. I fasted for 1 to 5 days at a time, with sometimes a 12-24 hour period where I did not ate or drank. During the 30-day period, food or fluids only touched my mouth on 8 different days, but I still was not free. In fact, the enemy knew I was trying to unseat him and I faced tremendous backlash. There were times when things were going great for a day or two, then I had a dream or vision about being in water, being fed, intimate contact, etc. and was placed back in bondage. It sounded so easy when Jesus said some devils only come out by prayer and fasting (Matthew 17:21). I was willing to fast for 100 days straight if necessary, but I wanted it to end when I finished the fast.

Ministers cannot afford to let pride into their heart. Despite their gifts and calling, pride may cause the Lord to withhold even more information from them. **Never forget, the Lord is God.** Elisha had an incredible prophetic ministry, coupled with signs and wonders. He wanted to bless the Shunammite woman who had been a blessing to him. When he found out that she had no children, the Scriptures do not indicate if Elisha inquired of the Lord or interceded on her behalf. The prophet simply said, *'About this season, according to the time of life, thou shalt embrace a son.'* ~ 2 Kings 4:16. He did not even use the Lord's name, but the prophecy came to pass (2 Kings 4:17). If he said something and the Lord backed him up by fulfilling it, such authority indicates an incredible relationship with the Lord. We all have to continually seek and remain in communion with Christ Jesus. Yet, despite Elisha's relationship with the Lord, and the resultant authority, when the Shunammite's son later died, take note of what Elisha said:

> "And when she came to the man of God to the hill, she caught him by the feet: but Gehazi came near to thrust her away. And the man of God said, *'Let her alone; for her soul is vexed within her:* ***and the Lord hath hid it from me, and hath not told me.***" ~ 2 Kings 4:27

A person who thinks he or she can use a gift as he or she pleases is on a collision course with serious error, embarrassment, and/or disappointment. Again, many gifted people tried to set me free but failed. It is indicative of despite how much we may want to take initiative at times that it is always best to do as the Lord commands. People fail but God does not fail. A part of being conformed into the image of Christ Jesus is approaching the ministry in the same way He did, to include staying within a certain region. My spiritual gifts work best when I am doing the Lord's will. When the Lord commissions a minister, He will assign the minister to a region. For example, the Lord sent Moses to Egypt (Exodus 3:10), Jeremiah to the nations (Jeremiah 1:5), and Ezekiel to the house of Israel (Ezekiel 2:3). Our authority is greatest within our jurisdiction, and when we remain rooted in the True Vine, Christ Jesus.

Recidivism Without Sin

I did not like it when after fasting, praying, constantly studying the Bible, and living holy, that the deliverance process was so painfully slow. Based on firsthand experience, I now know I should not assume that a person who does not receive a radical deliverance and remains free is at enmity with the Lord. I had deliverance ministers cast devils out of me, prayed for a fresh infilling of the Holy Spirit, and I felt liberated. I would not engage in sin and yet would get infected again as soon as I went to sleep, and absolutely no one could tell me why this kept happening over and over again. I felt like someone who had been wrongfully accused of a crime, jailed pending the arraignment, get released, begin celebrating as I walked down the courthouse steps, only to get arrested again on trumped up charges. I used to wonder how long it was going to take the Judge to say enough of this nonsense. After all, Jesus said, *'If the Son therefore shall make you free, ye shall be free indeed.'* ~ John 8:36. Arguably, the only thing worse than being in bondage is getting a slight taste of freedom then get incarcerated again. It was annoying, and even demoralizing at times, going through this process over and over again, wondering why the devil was able to get away with this for so long.

Sin Lets The Devil In (Sin Has Consequences)

The blood of Jesus cleanses us from all sin (1 John 1:7), but that does not mean we will not suffer the consequences of our actions. The wages of sin is death (Romans 6:23), so anything less than that is an example of God's love, exemplified through His mercy and grace. The God of the Old Covenant (Testament) sometimes gets the bad reputation of being unmerciful. However, God does not change (Malachi 3:6), and He has always been merciful, even in the way He slew an animal to cover Adam and Eve after they had sinned (Genesis 3:21). We also see God's loving mercy and justice in His judgment of David, after the Bathsheba and Uriah incident as indicated below:

"And David said unto Nathan, *'I have sinned against the Lord.'*

"And Nathan said unto David, *'The Lord also hath put away thy sin; thou shalt not die.'"* ~ 2 Samuel 12:13

The Lord spared David's life, even during his son Absalom's rebellion, but He did not spare David from suffering the severe consequences of his sinful actions. We can see why David said about the Lord, "…Thy rod and Thy staff they comfort me." ~ Psalm 23:4. The Lord's rod is an instrument of discipline, and we need to remember that the Lord rebukes those whom He loves (see Hebrews 12:5-11, Revelation 3:19). A sign of maturity, or at least heading in that direction, is when confronted with the consequences of our actions, no matter how painful they may be, or seemingly unfair to our repentant heart, we can say, "It is good for me that I have been afflicted; that I might learn Thy statutes." ~ Psalm 119:71

Witchcraft's Limits

The devil will gladly do everything within his limited power to help people accomplish their selfish goals via witchcraft. The devil's rebellion against God led to him being condemned to the worst imaginable punishment. Consequently, he has nothing to lose by helping to get us condemned too for joining his rebellion. There are various ways we can engage in witchcraft. For example, a spouse who pouts or uses sexual intimacy to manipulate his or her partner is engaging in witchcraft. The same applies to an errant minister who says, *'Touch not Mine anointed, and do My prophets no harm'* (1 Chronicles 16:22/Psalm 105:15) to intimidate others from holding him or her accountable. I do not know what these people are planning on saying to Jesus on judgment day, but a professing Christian who has an altar dedicated to another god, with a physical article as a point of contact to a targeted individual, possibly while conjuring demons and commissioning them to afflict that person, is engaging in witchcraft. Please heed the following regarding witchcraft:

> "Now the works of the flesh are manifest, which are these; Adultery, fornication, uncleanness, lasciviousness, idolatry, **witchcraft**, hatred, variance, emulations, wrath, strife, seditions, heresies, envyings, murders, drunkenness, revellings, and such like: of the which I tell you before, as I have also told you in time past, that **they which do such things shall not inherit the kingdom of God**." ~ Galatians 5:19-21

> "But the fearful, and unbelieving, and the abominable, and murderers, and whoremongers, and **sorcerers**, and idolaters, and all liars, **shall have their part in the lake which burneth with fire and brimstone: which is the second death**." ~ Revelation 21:8

> "And Samuel said, *'Hath the Lord as great delight in burnt offerings and sacrifices, as in obeying the voice of the Lord? Behold, to obey is better than sacrifice, and to hearken than the fat of rams.* **For rebellion is as the sin of witchcraft, and stubbornness is as iniquity and idolatry.** *Because thou hast rejected the word of the Lord, he hath also rejected thee from being king.'"* ~ 1 Samuel 15:22-23

> "Thus saith the Lord of hosts, the God of Israel; *'Ye have seen all the evil that I have brought upon Jerusalem, and upon all the cities of Judah; and, behold, this day* **they are a desolation, and no man dwelleth therein, Because of their wickedness which they have committed to provoke Me to anger, in that they went to burn incense, and to serve other gods, whom they knew not, neither they, ye, nor your fathers.** *Howbeit I sent unto you all My servants the prophets, rising early and sending them, saying, 'Oh, do not this abominable thing that I hate.' But they hearkened not, nor inclined their ear to turn from their wickedness, to burn no incense unto other gods. Wherefore My fury and Mine anger was poured forth, and was kindled in the cities of Judah and in the streets of Jerusalem; and they are wasted and desolate, as at this day. Therefore now thus saith the Lord, the God of hosts, the God of Israel; 'Wherefore commit ye this great evil against your souls, to cut off from you man and woman, child and*

suckling, out of Judah, to leave you none to remain; In that ye provoke Me unto wrath with the works of your hands, burning incense unto other gods in the land of Egypt, whither ye be gone to dwell, that ye might cut yourselves off, and that ye might be a curse and a reproach among all the nations of the earth? Have ye forgotten the wickedness of your fathers, and the wickedness of the kings of Judah, and the wickedness of their wives, and your own wickedness, and the wickedness of your wives, which they have committed in the land of Judah, and in the streets of Jerusalem? They are not humbled even unto this day, neither have they feared, nor walked in My law, nor in My statutes, that I set before you and before your fathers.' Therefore thus saith the Lord of hosts, the God of Israel; 'Behold, I will set My face against you for evil, and to cut off all Judah." ~ Jeremiah 44:2-11

The devil wants our soul, by any means necessary. Yet his collection of souls is like a person who dies and leaves behind a car collection. Even if the cars are buried with the person, they are of no further use. **All these souls the devil is collecting is ultimately useless to him. In the end, the devil is heaping up further judgment on himself and he will be too busy getting tormented to torment anyone (Revelation 20:10).** Likewise, he will help others obtain things they cannot retain, which will become a source of pain and embarrassment. Witchcraft has its limits, such as a shelf life, and because of this, there is the need for greater levels of more deviant sacrifices.

Remarkably, David had paid the price numerous times over for the right to marry king Saul's daughter. When Saul drove David into exile, causing him to leave his wife Michal behind, without divorcing her, Saul gave Michal to another man. After Saul's passing and David was enthroned as the king over Hebron, he had one request prior to his rise to the king over Israel. He wanted Michal, his wife for whom he had paid the price (2 Samuel 3). When David's messengers told Saul's son Ishbosheth to return David's first wife, Phaltiel, Michal's new (yet illegitimate) husband, followed behind her in tears. One could say David had other wives, and since it appears that Phaltiel loved Michal, David could have let him keep her. But let us examine a few things. David had paid a tremendous price to marry Michal. He killed Goliath, which was all that was needed. But Saul, in an attempt to have David killed, said he would accept a dowry of 100 philistine foreskins. David could not have convinced even one Philistine to let him circumcise him, which meant David had to kill 100 Philistines to get their foreskins. Yet, David exceeded the standards by killing 200 Philistines. It did not matter how many wives David had, He was not going to let anyone have anything he worked so hard and risked his life to have. You may have heard people say that what God has for you is for you. So, similarly to David, I depend on the Lord to not allow anyone to use witchcraft to hijack a blessing He has ordained and promised to me. Witchcraft is potentially effective but it becomes a source of embarrassment for the devil and the witch when the Lord intervenes.

The devil may also set a person up for embarrassment to obtain something he or she cannot keep. The coveted item becomes bait to lead a person towards greater damnation, and to harvest more souls. Heartbreakingly, some people are paying a price because an ancestor made a deal with the devil. You may find it unfathomable to sell yourself or any member of your family to the devil, for anything. Conversely, your ancestors may have been desperate and/or selfish. The devil has a history of showing up in a person's life at the greatest moment of desperation. Like an angel of light, he offers a "solution", a way of escape that puts a person in bondage to him, a plan of damnation dressed as a plan of redemption. It may have seemed harmless for Jesus to take the devil's advice by turning the stone into bread. On the surface, it seemed like a good plan because Jesus was starving. But it would have caused Jesus to sin, thereby tarnishing His ability to serve as the sinless perfection needed to atone for the sins of the world. It was not written during the Lord's tribulation, but in accordance with Romans 6:16, what we obey becomes our lord.

Many people have succumbed to the devil's knack for using desperation as a source of a person's inspiration. Can you imagine if Phaltiel had challenged king David's rights to Michal? He could have said David had abandoned Michal while, he, Phaltiel, showed unwavering and unfailing love to Michal so he was more suited for her. Therefore, she should be rightfully his. These are the thought processes the devil has instilled in people, and that is why some have tried to use witchcraft to obtain things the Lord has denied them.

THE PROCESS: THE REFINER'S FIRE

Why Witchcraft?

Practicing witchcraft comes with a one-way nonrefundable ticket to hell for those who refuse to repent (Galatians 5:19-21, Revelation 21:8). So, why would anyone want to practice witchcraft? The short answer is, "plausible deniability". Witchcraft allows a person, whether the practitioner or client, to do dirty deeds while seemingly maintaining clean hands. Hence, some people would never suspect their grandparent or even their pastor is practicing witchcraft. Overall, **witchcraft is imposing one's will on another person, even if it means trying to usurp the Lord's will for that person**. Practicing witchcraft puts the practitioner and/or client at enmity with God.

Many people are unknowingly practicing witchcraft because there are many types and levels of witchcraft. A basic level and type of witchcraft is a person who manipulates others by using the Scriptures. Praying against or outside of the Lord's will constitutes practicing witchcraft. A common example is a couple that is having either marital problems or may have gotten divorced. The Lord hates divorce (Malachi 2:16). Consequently, **many people have presumptuously engaged in marriage restoration prayers, even though it was not the Lord's will to restore the marriage**. You may wonder why God hates divorce but would not want to restore a marriage. Well, Solomon went astray and started following other gods because of some of his wives and concubines (1 Kings 11). It would have been wiser for Solomon to put away or divorce those women instead of staying with them and following other gods (devils). In some cases, the Lord may not want a couple to stay together because it was never His will to begin with. The continued union may also have detrimental long-term effects on one or both individuals. In addition, the Lord may not want the couple back together because the union was a "Demonically Arranged Union". Such a union was a product of witchcraft, the subversion of one person's will and destiny. The Lord will not support witchcraft and its fruit. Please note, praying outside of the Lord's will, may intentionally or inadvertently conjure devils that will try to answer the prayers, for a price. The devils will covertly forge a covenant and gain access to the family down to the third and fourth generations. At the highest levels of witchcraft, a person knowingly conjures devils, or may have devils assigned to him or her. Regardless of how much a devil does for a person, that devil's loyalty is to satan. The human is simply a hell-bound disposable vessel.

People get indoctrinated into witchcraft in various ways. Some start by being manipulative, and as desperation sets in, the pressure to accomplish a goal opens them up to resorting to deeper and darker levels of witchcraft in an effort to get things done. Consequently, it can be dangerous when a person refuses to take no for an answer, does not consider failure as an option, and is willing to accomplish a goal by any means necessary. Those things let the devil know the individual welcomes his "assistance". You may have heard entertainers seemingly jokingly speak of selling their souls to the devil, but they are deadly serious. In some cases, they might have had an encounter with the devil or one of his emissaries, where they sold their soul to the devil in exchange for fame and fortune. Every demonic covenant requires a sacrifice, some more appalling than others.

In Genesis 15 for example, the Lord had Abraham sacrifice animals in order to form a covenant with Him. Nowadays, we do not need to sacrifice animals to God because Christ Jesus became the ultimate sacrifice. In fact, in accordance with Galatians 3:13-14, Christ became a sacrifice for us (Gentile believers) so we can benefit from that Abrahamic covenant. On the contrary, the devil requires goods or services in order for a person to make a covenant with him. Ultimately, the devil will require a blood sacrifice, payable immediately upon making a covenant, during its lifespan, or upon its expiration. In some cases, an entertainer can sell his or her soul to the devil in exchange for fame, or at least promised fame, and the devil will do his part to give the person the desires of his or her heart. Sadly, a part of that blood covenant with the devil is he will kill the individual at the end of the covenant, or if the person breeches the covenant, so the person will go to hell, unless he or she turns to Jesus. That is a part of why you will see someone who lacks talent in an area, yet he or she enjoys a great measure of "success". The devil uses his infrastructure to give a person the success he or she desires, and that includes a large and loyal social media following to give a person unprecedented fame. A time inevitably comes when a person realizes the magnitude of the demonic covenant, and that it was not worth it, which is when the feeling of doom sets in. Some people know they can give it all up and turn to Christ Jesus for redemption and salvation, which is what they do. Others may see Jesus as an option but do not want to give up the benefits of the demonic covenant. Then there are those who think there is no escaping the demonic covenant although there is redemptive power in the blood of Jesus.

On many occasions, the devil makes promises without fulfilling them. But that is one of the risks a person takes when he or she makes a deal with a thief, a liar, and a hypocrite who will hold the person to everything he or she promised to do. Sometimes the person may become a "one hit wonder", which the devil can use to say he completed his part of the deal. Now, if the person wants a greater measure and duration of fame, it will require a sacrifice of a greater magnitude. This is how and why sometimes a friend or family member gets killed. Ultimately, the devil is after a blood sacrifice. Another option is to do something embarrassing. The public humiliation is like a pledge of allegiance to the devil. Once a person forges a covenant with the devil, the individual becomes like a fish on a hook that is controlled by the enemy's line. The covenant will require periodic sacrifices of greater levels. Consequently, sometimes an entertainer may start off looking like a young man or woman straight from a church choir, but by the time the enemy is done transforming that individual, well, it does not look good. The person ends up looking like a demon in the flesh, and a walking billboard for the devil. Those who get into witchcraft will also have to make sacrifices for increased power and authority in the kingdom of darkness.

After that detour, let us get back to the plausible deniability aspects of engaging in witchcraft. A professing Christian, who is actually a witch (on some level), can praise the Lord in church every time the doors are open as a way to create a cover. Jesus compared the Pharisees and scribes to whitewashed sepulchers, full of dead men's bones (Matthew 23:27-28). Their holiness was aesthetic at best. Likewise, many professing Christians, whether a part of the clergy or the laity, look holy on the outside but are dark on the inside. People who lack discernment will simply focus on the polished veneer of the pretender. Jesus said the mouth speaks what the heart is full of (Matthew 12:34). However, while the person may speak about Jesus, a lot, we should examine the person's fruits. Look at what drives the person to anger and even how easily he or she gets angry. Does the person forgive his or her enemies? Can the person pray for the Lord to bless his or her enemies, and rejoice if the Lord blesses the adversary? Sometimes it takes subtle hints to realize a person is like veneer that is covering rotten teeth. Do not let anyone cause you to turn your discernment off. Unbelievably, some churchgoers are practicing the highest levels of witchcraft. Some are in leadership or influential positions, which outwardly makes it unfathomable that they are engaging in witchcraft.

Some people engage in witchcraft because they can do things behind closed doors that are oftentimes difficult to prove. For example, a person who is having bad dreams may not be able to definitively prove that the dreams are coming from the pastor. This is because the pastor preaches Holy Spirit fire in the pulpit, but is secretly conjuring devils in his house or is doing soul travel to keep the congregation in bondage. The pastor engages in witchcraft possibly based on the desire to have a sizable congregation. The pastor may discourage congregants from even visiting other churches. This is however, a form of control masked as concern. The devil, who masquerades as an angel of light, has ensnared many ministers with promises to help them do greater works for the Lord. Regrettably, they end up serving the devil instead. Witchcraft also provides the seemingly perfect cover for someone who is not willing to confront issues with another person directly. Therefore, they try to attack the individual in the spiritual realm. However, God is watching and He is everywhere.

The potential power associated with witchcraft lures some people. While the Holy Spirit gives gifts as He wills, the devil basically empowers a person in accordance with the level and amount of sacrifices they are willing to make to him. Therefore, sometimes it seems as if a worker of iniquity is more powerful than a Christian. Heartbreakingly, some ministers with struggling ministries have resorted to demonic powers to give themselves a boost. As previously stated, the gifts of the Holy Spirit are not in accordance with a person's self-will. So, despite popular belief, a person cannot prophesy at will because such a "prophecy" is not from the Lord. A person can make a proclamation in the name of the Lord, but if the Lord did not inspire the message, He is not obligated to bring it to pass. On the contrary, if a person is making a false prophecy on behalf of the devil, and the intended recipient comes in agreement with it, the devil has permission to bring the prophecy to pass. An example of this is a false prophet can prophesy that someone will get married within a specified time, and if the person believes the prophecy, he or she is actually giving the devil permission to bring the prophecy to pass by matching the person with a spouse of the devil's choosing. In such cases, the marriage will be miserable, and oftentimes destined for divorce. Again, the devil frequently helps people to get what they want but they either will not be able to keep, or it will cost them everything to keep. The subsequent embarrassment is for the devil's entertainment, but it also pressures the person to make greater sacrifices to the devil in an effort to gain redemption. The devil tries to be a father to disenfranchised people and use their rejection to lure them into practicing witchcraft. It is dangerous to desire success as a way of getting back at others who did not treat you well in the past. One of the drawbacks to that mindset, which leads to greater levels of resentment, is they may not respect you regardless of your level of success. Hence, witchcraft puts people in bondage to the devil. Tragically, for some people, witchcraft is a family business that has produced fruit on the family tree for generations. They do not know better than to practice witchcraft because it is in their blood.

Nepotism is a part of witchcraft. Therefore, it should not come as a surprise when a child of a witch becomes a witch. Sadly, some children are infused with demons in their mother's womb and are literally children of the devil. One of the reasons why some people suffer intense spiritual warfare is because they have broken away from the family tradition of practicing witchcraft. The enemy does not like to lose, and he sees the person as his rightful property because of his investment into the family, possibly for many centuries. When parents dedicate children to the devil, he will vigorously pursue the children to get them to serve him or perish. One of the reasons to pay attention to our dreams is the enemy may try to indoctrinate us into witchcraft while we sleep. It is no joke to have a dream about being on an altar or in the midst of a pentagram with people gathered around, most likely shrouded in darkness, for a ceremony. Such an individual cannot afford to be a lukewarm Christian. Tragically, some people inadvertently dedicated their children to the devil by consulting witches, such as tarot card readers, mediums and psychics regarding the birth of a desired child.

There is no escaping from the Lord (see Psalm 139). Yet, somehow, many professing Christians seemingly forget the Lord sees everything, and He will hold them accountable for everything they do including things they did in the dark. Ephesians 5:11 clearly instructs us to "…have no fellowship with the unfruitful works of darkness, but rather reprove them." We have a similar caution in 1 Corinthians 10:20-22, which states, "Ye cannot drink the cup of the Lord, and the cup of devils: ye cannot be partakers of the Lord's table, and of the table of devils. Do we provoke the Lord to jealousy? Are we stronger than He?" [*By the way, the latter Scripture points to some of the SINinster things about eating or being fed in a demonic dream. It could serve as initiation into witchcraft, or, cause you to violate the Word of God by partaking in the things of the devil. And when you sin, you let the devil in. The devil's level of desperation and aggressiveness increase as his time gets shorter.*] A professing Christian is no longer engaging in witchcraft from a place of ignorance when any of the following abominations are in play:

- Created an altar, even allegedly dedicated to the Lord, but is praying against people's God-ordained destinies.
- Chanting, burning incense and pouring out drink offerings to the gods.
- Making sacrifices, especially blood sacrifices, to other gods.
- Sticking pins into a voodoo doll
- Writing a person's name down, cursing it, and…
- Conjuring devils to project them towards others, in part to make it seem as if God has brought judgment on them.

Some professing Christians have used witchcraft to kill people and showed up at their funeral, grieving as if they have no idea what happened to the deceased. This will not make some people feel well, but based on personal near-death experiences, some people who seemingly passed away peacefully in their sleep did not. A witch showed up at my house to see if her spells to make me sick had worked. It may have seemed cute to some, but the witch brought a gift bag shortly before my birthday. But I was not going to accept a "gift" from a witch. Likewise, be careful whom you except "gifts" from, including food because it may serve as a point of contact for them to project demons towards you. That is why, at the end of a relationship, it is important to discard things associated with your former partner. Therefore, do not fight over the furniture during divorce proceedings. Also, if you were fornicating or in an adulterous relationship, the bed used for intimacy spiritually became a satanic altar.

Engaging in witchcraft is dangerous in many ways. One of the gifts of the Holy Spirit is the discerning of spirits. Some people can spot a witch a mile away because of a revelation from the Lord. They will not require any evidence, but the Lord will confirm the revelation. The Lord reveals a person's true character in many ways. In the case of the witch who showed up at my door, one of the ways the Lord revealed her true nature was by giving someone else a dream about her. The dreamer saw the witch, who is posing as a Christian, in a pit surrounded by snakes. However, instead of the snakes being a threat, she was controlling them. While snakes may represent liars, those who tell tales, like how snakes have long tails, they may also represent devils. We see this when the devil approached Eve in the Garden of Eden cloaked as a snake. The Book of Revelation refers to the devil as the old serpent and a dragon. The serpent is representative of the deceiver, while the dragon is the accuser of the brethren. Among many the dreams or visions I have had, there were times when I saw snakes and dragons. Despite the number of demonic dreams or visions, I did not ask the Lord to shut down my ability to see things in the spiritual realm, which was one of the enemy's objectives. It was better to have them and be able to see what the enemy was doing, or trying to do, rather than not have them and be spiritually blind. Some may consider ignorance bliss, but that is not prudent when it comes to knowing about the devil's devices.

Astral projection (soul travel) is one of the covert devices some workers of iniquity use. There were times when the Lord translated Elijah, Ezekiel, and Philip the evangelist from one location to the other. Soul travel is a perversion of that and is based on a person's will or an assignment from the devil. Unlike those men who went on assignments for the Lord, soul travellers usually go out to do evil deeds. So, someone may live with a witch and think the person is asleep because the body is present. However, because of the person's will, or demonic assignment, the person's soul may have departed from the body and is away doing evil deeds. Some people use soul travel to cast curses, spy on others, commit sexual assault and even rape. Thankfully, the Lord sees all, and He is a God of righteousness and judgment.

The Lord took the prophet Ezekiel into the inner sanctum of people's lives and exposed their evil deeds (Ezekiel 8). While it may be hard to prove that a person is engaging in witchcraft, if the Lord exposes it to one of His prophets, the Lord may have the prophet impose judgment on the worker of iniquity. Failure to repent oftentimes results in public exposure. Now, for as much grace as I will extend to my enemies, as you may recall, my policy is "If it flies, it dies." It is up to the Lord to honor that request, but I am not friendly with anyone who would dare astral project to defile or destroy a person's life.

Many people erroneously believe New Testament prophets only deliver good news. While the gospel is the good news (of Christ Jesus), prophets will have to impose judgment as declared from the Lord. Joseph did not have any biases towards his fellow prisoners; he simply gave them the Word of the Lord. He spoke of the cupbearer's restoration in three days and the baker's death. The Lord sent Isaiah to tell king Hezekiah to put his house in order because he was going to die. Jeremiah also told the prophet Hananiah he was going to die by the end of the year for teaching rebellion against the Lord. The prophet Hananiah died within two months as a result of the Lord's judgment. For those who want to say those examples are from the Old Testament, the prophet Agabus told Paul people were going to arrest him. Also, the Book of Revelation is filled with the most unpleasant prophecies. Prophecy is not about making someone feel good, especially while they are in sin. It is about delivering the Word of the Lord, which oftentimes includes a call to repentance. Prophecy is not about giving feel-good messages; it is about bringing people to holiness, and a righteous relationship with Christ Jesus. Remember, '...*The testimony of Jesus is the Spirit of Prophecy.*' ~ Revelation 19:10

Never forget that judgment begins in the house of God (1 Peter 4:17). This is a strong warning to those in the house of God who are practicing witchcraft as if God is not watching, and that He will not hold them accountable for their evil deeds. The Lord gives people time to repent, but if they do not, judgment will come. Things done in the dark will be shouted from the rooftops. Many people take the Lord's period of grace as approval of their actions, seemingly not knowing their condemnation draws nigh lest they repent. Jesus spoke of *'greater damnation'*. That is what Christians, especially ministers, who are practicing witchcraft will get if they do not repent for partnering with the devil while pretending to love and serve Christ Jesus. A person can try all forms of schemes to deny engaging in witchcraft. However, none of those schemes will work when the person stands before the judgment seat of Christ Jesus.

There is a place called hell! No one can say they ended up in hell because Jesus was an unrighteous judge. Even if a person were to accuse Jesus of unrighteousness, who is that person going to appeal the Lord's decision to. The devil cannot override Jesus' authority. The Father has given all power and authority to His Son, Jesus the Christ, to judge all of His creation, which includes the devil, who is already damned. It is an awful thing to know and preach the Word of God while defying it in the confines of your home, or wherever your altar is, such as in a Freemason Lodge. The Lord sees your evil altars and evil deeds. Unless you repent, you will perish and suffer in hell, followed by the lake of fire, where you and the devil you serve will be tormented forever and ever. So, whereas I began this section by speaking of why witchcraft, I pray that you also see the reasons not engaging in witchcraft. Nothing the devil has to offer is worth keeping. The devil can only truly offer death and hell; he can only take you where he is certainly going. Please remain mindful of the fact that the Lord created hell for the devil and his angels.

The Devil is a Thief

Being embroiled in spiritual warfare takes time away from praising the Lord, reading and studying the Bible and spending time with the Lord. The devil is trying to do the impossible by defying when Jesus said, *'And I give unto them eternal life; and they shall never perish, neither shall any man pluck them out of my hand. My Father, which gave them Me, is greater than all; and no man is able to pluck them out of My Father's hand. I and My Father are one.'* ~ John 10:28-30. While he will not admit to it, the devil knows he cannot win so he is content with settling for being an absolute nuisance. The devil will try to steal as much of our time and attention from the Lord as possible. There is danger in focusing too much on the devil. On the contrary, it is dangerous to ignore him. The tag line for Social Aloe Ministries is "Glorifying God. Exposing the devil." I have to ensure that exposing the devil does not prevent me from glorifying the Lord. You may have heard some people say even bad publicity is good publicity. In recent years, look at how every attempt (to date) to bring Donald Trump down has backfired. The negative things used against him, even things that were seemingly going to be the nail in his coffin, ended up giving him a boost in publicity. Similarly, with the help of the Holy Spirit, do not spend too much time trying to expose the devil. Spending time with the Lord, a God of Light, makes it easier to identify darkness. Some people have spent too much time in the darkness, doing "research", trying to expose or even shame the devil. One of the inherent dangers of such a "ministry" is making it seem as if the devil is more powerful than the Lord. Before calling me a hypocrite, there were times I was reluctant to write this book because of its darkness, but I must expose what I experienced and learned while in the dark.

I am gracious for the many times during my tribulation when the Lord discreetly let me know He was still present, and very much in control. For example, I experienced numerous roadblocks when I tried delivering a message the Lord had given to me in a vision. Yet, in 2016, on a trip to Jamaica, I was amazed how He brought me together with a lady who was vacationing from the United Kingdom. Numerous obstacles could have prevented that encounter, but the Lord is Sovereign and He had given me an assignment. There was also another encounter with someone else in Jamaica where we walked by each other, until the Lord turned things around. That incident is reminiscent of my 2013 trip to Australia. The Lord let me know on the first night of my two-week stay that He had three people for me to meet. One of them had walked by me but then turned around and started walking towards me. There were times when it was demoralizing to know the Lord could send me to these countries, and then bring me together with people for me to minister to them. However, there were too many challenges for me to release a life-altering message to His daughter. It reminded me of when Elijah said it would not rain or dew until he gave the Word. Consequently, there was a 3.5-year drought in Israel. I felt bad for the young lady, as if her life was being put on hold. Yet, which is also another lesson learned, it is not good to resort to witchcraft while trying to do the work of the Lord. There is danger in delivering a prophecy too late or too soon. As a messenger of the Lord, it is not our responsibility to manipulate or force a person to receive the Word of the Lord. We also have to be careful about trying to tear down walls that may be blocking us from delivering that message. Bear in mind that the God who made a way for Moses to appear before the pharaoh, to deliver the Word of the Lord, can certainly give us an audience with the desired recipient whenever He chooses. Mindfully, the Lord may give us a message for someone who will reject us, and subsequently our message, to his or her detriment. The Lord sent prophets, to include Jeremiah, to warn the nation of Israel so they would not have to spend 70 years in captivity. They ignored and even disobeyed the prophets. Learn to recognize when to cease our efforts, lest we venture into "prophetic witchcraft". We should not allow the devil manipulate us into trying to manipulate others because we want to do something for their benefit. Remember that freewill is a double-edged sword…

Submitting to God and resisting a devil does not always mean he will flee immediately (James 4:7). When Jesus resisted the devil's temptation to turn a rock into bread, many would think the devil already knew Jesus was the Son of God so he would leave Jesus alone, but the devil persisted. Some may reason that since the devil only tried to tempt Jesus three times, based on the three portals of sin (lust of the flesh, lust of the eyes, and the pride of life ~ 1 John 2:16), that messengers of satan only attack thrice and then leave. That is not the case, especially when we might have a devil assigned to us, one who will face tremendous "disciplinary actions" within the kingdom of darkness for failing. The devil will go to tremendous depths, lengths, and breadths to wear its target down and eventually out. Many can attest to dating different people who all share the same bad trait(s). Some have attributed this, and often rightfully so, to the same devil showing up cloaked in a different person. Unfortunately, sometimes the overlooked cause is the one who continually makes poor choices for a variety of issues.

Some people erroneously think resisting the devil is simply ignoring him. However, think about eating some fries when a pesky fly shows up. First you try swatting it away but it keeps coming back. Then it seems as if the fly is more interested in you than the fries, as if it knows it is beginning to work on your last nerve. One way to test this is to put a fry off to the side where the fly can feast on it and you won't bother it, in part so it won't bother you. However, as you may know based on firsthand experience, the fly will still try to attack the rest of your fries, and subsequently, you. In the same vein, ignoring the devil will not make him go away. Making concessions to him is not effective either. The principles in James 4:7 require full submission to the Lord and total resistance to the enemy. Do not give the enemy any room to operate in your life. I like the analogy that if a person who is driving a car stops to pick up the devil, the devil will end up driving. In addition, he will eventually lock the person away in the trunk with seemingly no way to escape or regain control. If you are in such a dark and confined position, it is not hopeless. Jonah was in a similar situation, but he cried out to the Lord who delivered the wayward prophet. As it is written, "And it shall come to pass, that **whosoever shall call on the name of the Lord shall be delivered**: for in mount Zion and in Jerusalem shall be deliverance, as the Lord hath said, and in the remnant whom the Lord shall call." ~ Joel 2:32. Jesus used the name beelzebub in one of His rebukes to the Pharisees (Matthew 12). The name means "lord of the flies", which aptly describes the annoying similarities between devils and flies.

Pay attention to the spiritual realm. There was a time when I felt like I was not receiving as many visions from the Lord when compared to dreams. However, the attacks made me realize I was having more visions than I was paying attention to. While a dream requires a person to be asleep, a vision can occur while awake or asleep, with eyes open or closed. Like As stated, there were times when I came under attack after closing my eyes for a few seconds. It was like suddenly closing my eyes and falling into the pits of hell. Yet, it was as if I was "just seeing things", until I had to deal with the physical manifestations. The other side of paying attention to the spirit world was how things seemed peaceful, appearing as if no evil spirits were lurking. However, the Lord revealed things through the five supernatural senses, which mirror our five natural senses. This was a part of the Lord's answer to my desire that I articulated in a post in 2015. I was inspired to write that many people say the world needs more love, but I argued that it needed more discernment. I also wanted more discernment to help distinguish good from evil. I thought, or I should say I wanted, the Lord to give me an increased level of the gift of the discerning of spirits. Instead, He exposed me to evil for a while, which gave me invaluable practical experiences.

The enemy attacked me thousands of times in dreams and visions. Moreover, he also used people, some of who were like pawns in a game they did not realize they were playing. For example, a pastor wanted to shake my hand. I initially declined but he persisted. He was old enough to be my father and I did not want to disrespect him, so I obliged. Sadly, I had been delivered until that handshake forged a demonic covenant, which left me with that despised feeling in my left side, again. I got a taste of why Peter said something to Jesus who responded by rebuking the devil

(Matthew 16:22-23). There were times when I was sitting for example and someone who had never touched me before, "somehow" had the desire to maybe touch me on my shoulder. Then the devil came back, like that pesky fly. As a result, I have learned to be very careful about who I come in contact with, especially until I know the Lord has restored my shield of protection against such demonic infestation. I prefer to prevent things instead of trying to get delivered from it. The devil is dogged and sneaky.

Dirty Boxing

I went to a deliverance seminar where the instructor likened demons to rats, and humans to a house. The premise was rats are more attracted and comfortable in dirty homes. As a result, one of the ways to get rid of the rats is by cleaning the house, which means to repent of our sins. While that premise sounds great, I also discovered, through practical experiences, that when a "rat" likes a "house", it will attempt to bring trash into the house to claim it has a right to the house, and to make itself feel more at home. It is a dirty technique, which I liken to a branch of MMA referred to as "dirty boxing". It is a form of guerrilla warfare, which are creative measures oftentimes used against a superior force where an open confrontation is ill-advised. That is a part of the reason why the enemy usually attacked when I was asleep, and to a lesser extent, when I was tired and closed my eyes to rest.

Whenever I had a dream of a sexual nature, it was not because I had been out staring at women or watching pornography, or even thinking about sex. So, because I was not doing those things, the enemy brought those things to me. There were times when I was having a sexual dream and did not realize until it was done. The enemy wanted me to forge covenants with him, and since I would not, he basically illegally obtained my signature on a legal document. It gave me a feeling of being arrested by a law enforcement officer who was so desperate to make an arrest that he or she planted evidence on me. I recall waking up from a dream where I was sexually assaulted while Psalm 55 was playing. Another assault took place in my sleep while the narrator was reading one of the gospels. In fact, one of the first things I heard the narrator say when I woke up was the name of Jesus. A part of me revealing the above is because people may tell us to fill our homes with the Word of God to keep the devils out. Well, they attacked me while I was filling up on the Word of God.

Some people have never experienced these levels of attacks because, like Job, the Lord protects them, whether they are righteous or not. But for others, also like Job, they are attacked for their righteousness. In addition, they are fully committed and therefore submitted to the Lord, and they consciously try to remove and shut the door on every source and type of sin. Sadly, rather than recognizing the person's righteousness and backing off, the enemy resorts to more devious methods. Consequently, such an individual will discover that the cleaner he or she gets is the dirtier the enemy fights. In some aspects, such a methodology seems very unfair, which it is. But as the saying goes, "New levels, new devils." One thing a believer should never do is resort to retaliating with the dirty methods the enemy uses, lest the believer becomes like the enemy, to include being at enmity with the Lord. We defeat the enemy's lies with the truth and his darkness with light.

Masking

I have performed thousands of hearing tests that included using a technique called "masking". It mimics trying to have a conversation while other people or objects are making noise in the area. While the person is listening for the test tone in the right ear for example, the masking noise is presented in the left ear. The noise is constant, which puts the tested individual in a position to miss the beeping pulsing tones in the tested ear, particularly if the person focuses too much on the masking noise. Similarly, I have had visions within a dream from the Lord before, or even a dream within a dream. Conversely, the enemy did such things to mask his evil deeds. For instance, I had a recent dream about driving around in a parking lot, looking for a parking spot. Then I realized I was also having a dream with sexual activity. While the dream could simply be about the sexual activity, even the "noise" in this case had a message that worked in concert and even independently of the sexual dream. Overall, the dream represented an attempted covenant with the devil for him to bring confusion, delay and waywardness into my life. For those who like the sexual activity in their dreams, you may get sexual pleasure in exchange for something that is far from pleasurable. Any form of sexual activity with a devil is not simply ungodly; it is potentially deadly. Sexual encounters with a devil are more dangerous than having unprotected sex with a prostitute at the end of his or her shift.

Owl

Owls are silent killers during the day and night. A mouse may not even hear the owl flapping its wings as it prepares to descend upon its intended prey. Even though the devil intentionally made noises in my house, there were times when it went into "stealth mode". However, the Lord would still alert me of things. A part of why the Lord did not allow me to see things most of the time was to help train my other spiritual senses. Unfortunately, one of the things I did not like was when the Lord gave me warnings but did not allow me to stop the attacks. When the Lord warned me of a pending attack, I usually wanted to surprise the devil as he pounced by thrusting it with a flaming hot sword into its chest and out through its skull. I wondered how the Lord would punish this devil for its attacks against me, and numerous other people it had afflicted throughout the ages. I absolutely hate this devil! Consequently, despite any warfare, I happily present the information contained therein to help do a part of what the Lord has called me to do, which is to set the captives (His children) free. It was painfully humorous when the Lord gave me that commission because my intense warfare suggested I was in bondage to the enemy. The devil is like a stealthy owl, but with the Lord's help, we can be aware of his presence or pending arrival.

Hot Potato

There are times when the devil tries pulling a really "fast one". For example, you may suddenly have a dream or vision where someone hands you a box, without you seeing who gave it to you. Or, maybe the dream or vision has someone, oftentimes a person whose face you cannot see, giving you a baby without you having time to process the information, to include if it is truly a child. The encounter only lasted a few seconds but leaves you wondering what in the world just happened. Well, the things that came into your possession was like playing a game of hot potato, except the enemy did not give you a chance to hand off whatever he gave to you, which leaves you stuck with it. When it comes to the enemy, whatever he is trying to force on you is not a game. Even if it were a game, he is not playing around.

Before throwing away the "hot potato", let us examine what the above situations may mean. In a lot of ways, a package is a "Trojan Horse". Despite its drab exterior, the devil is not going to give you a good gift. There is also a very sinister implication behind what you did not see in such a dream or vision. Before a delivery person can hand you a package, you need to open the door. Opening a door to the enemy is not done to simply see who is there. Oh no, that thieving lying devil takes the open door as your consent, or even your invitation, to come in to your life to destroy it. So, before willing or unwillingly accepting the package, the devil will claim you knowingly invited him and willingly accepted the package. Then, who knows what is in the box, which, by nature of being in your house, is free to afflict whoever is in your house with its contents. The contents may include chaos, confusion, debt, setback, strife, adultery, etc. I share these things to help you realize the potential severity of such seemingly innocuous dreams or visions, and why it is important to immediately reject and rebuke them in the name of Jesus, as well as to return them to the sender in the name of Jesus. You need to get rid the "package", preferably unopened, as soon as you realize what is going on. If the enemy gave you something in the spiritual realm, so by faith, immediately return it to him in the spiritual realm.

I need to state that despite any claims the devil makes against us, Jesus is a righteous judge. The Lord does not simply look at the fact that a covenant may have been formed with the devil; He also examines how a covenant was formed. One of the reasons why some of the devil's plans fail so miserably is because he often uses illegal moves to try to forge or maintain a (seemingly) legal covenant. It always helps to cry out to the Lord for immediate justice.

The other dream or vision I described had to do with a baby. Well, in real life, a baby requires our resources. It may require its mother's milk, which in this case, represents the devil stealing our virtues. The devil tries to steal the things the Lord placed in us for the growth and nourishment of others. For some people, the Lord had intended them to do "bigger and better" things but that old thief robbed them of their destiny, with their consent, due to ignorance of the devil's devices. Many persons have heard this very motivating Scripture: *'For I know the thoughts that I think toward you'*, saith the Lord, *'thoughts of peace, and not of evil, to give you an expected end.'* ~

Jeremiah 29:11. One of the reasons why those things may not have manifested in our life is because it is a plan of God instead of a promise from Him. The Lord has wonderful plans for people that are on hold because they knowingly or unknowingly have a contradictory covenant in effect with the devil that is robbing them of their God-ordained destiny. It is like the Lord having a wonderful spouse for someone but that person keeps getting into other relationships.

Okay, let us get back to the baby. A baby requires a lot of time and attention. That may manifest in your life in the form of you being busy, working hard, with nothing to show for it. A baby from the devil also requires a long-term commitment. It could be equivalent to signing an 18-year covenant with the devil for him to rob you during that time. There are times when I hear of two elderly people getting married, and the story seems touching. But sometimes I wonder if the Lord had intended for them to be together sooner but the devil kept using one or both of those individuals to block their own God-ordained destiny. I sometimes wonder if the enemy blocked their marriage because they were destined to give birth to a child whose ministry would change the world, for the better. Here is another cautionary note about a devil giving you a baby. If you have an offspring who is now a teenager, but the devil gives that offspring in the form of a baby, it is not good. You may wake up and think about how adorable your child was at that age. However, that old conman, the devil, is trying to give you a gift of backwardness. Also, because of our child's current age and stage, and how the child regressed, the enemy is trying to form a covenant with you to stop your progress to a certain level and then takes you back down and have to start over. There may be a very sinister reason behind why some people feel as if they take one step forward but end up going ten steps backwards. The devil may have implemented a blockade, a glass ceiling of sorts, on their ability to progress.

The enemy will try to give you these types of dreams over and over again to reinstate his covenants especially when he knows or discerns that you have a breakthrough on the way. The enemy will not attack some people in these ways based on their gifting from the Lord. I know of someone who has the gift to wake up from a dream, go back to sleep, and return to the dream right where she left off. Such a gifting means the dreamer can immediately hold the devil accountable and immediately reverse everything he just did. Some people have asked the Lord to give them that ability, and He may give it to them based on previous enemy attacks. Unfortunately for me during this season, there were no shortcuts or easy route. Even trying to undo the enemy's actions took a lot of praying, and sometimes, even then, it did not mean the Lord would break the enemy's evil covenants. Because of that, I can share these revelations.

Forgotten Dreams

A major part of having a rudimentary understanding of demonic dreams and visions is to develop a specific spiritual warfare strategy in response to them. The enemy's attacks leave him vulnerable to your counterattacks. When a person is ignorant of the devil's devices, the devil can openly operate with impunity because the person does not fully understand the potential ramifications. However, once a person gains wisdom into the enemy's operations, the devil will resort to more covert means of securing the person's corporation. [*By the way, I will use the word "dream" to represent both dreams and visions.*] One of those covert tactics is when the enemy induces a dream and then causes the individual to forget about the dream. The adversary may accomplish this by having something in the natural realm quickly wake the person up, like a distracting phone call. By the time the call is over, the dreamer forgets he or she had a dream, or at least the details of that dream.

Dreams are sometimes seemingly written in disappearing ink. As a result, the longer you wait to address them is the less you will recall the contents, or even worse, you may forget about the dream. Other techniques include basically wiping the dreamer's memory or giving a feint dream that goes by undetected. It is like the enemy turns a vehicle off, puts it in neutral, and then silently pushes it pass you so that you cannot perceive it because it did not make its traditional loud sound.

When it comes to assessing a person's vision, we often consider a visual acuity of 20/20 as being perfect. But some people can see better than 20/20, for example, some people have a visual acuity of 20/10. Likewise, a person who hears frequencies at levels between 0 decibels (dB) and 25dB is considered hearing within normal limits. However, it is possible for some people to hear at levels below 0dB. An audiologist may not be particularly concerned with testing to see exactly how well a person can hear, as long as the person can hear within normal limits. But the audiologist does have the ability to present a tone that is below 0dB. Likewise, when our spiritual senses are sharp, the enemy uses more covert techniques to try to get his dangerous payload by us.

The enemy is notorious for trying to corrupt and/or counterfeit the things of God. An example of this is when one of Job's friends, Elihu, gave the following powerful revelation:

> *'For God speaketh once, yea twice, **yet man perceiveth it not**. In a dream, in a vision of the night, when deep sleep falleth upon men, in slumberings upon the bed; Then He openeth the ears of men, and sealeth their instruction, That He may withdraw man from his purpose, and **hide pride from man**. He keepeth back his soul from the pit, and his life from perishing by the sword.'* ~ Job 33:14-18

Tragically, the devil tries to induce dreams a person cannot perceive, but his motives are sinister because his whole intent is to put the person in bondage to him. The person's failure to resist or rebuke the demonic dream forges a covenant. However, a dream from the Lord does not require us to come into agreement with it. In fact, we can rebuke it and it will not matter. Others can try to stop it from coming to pass but they will fail. When the Lord gives a person a prophetic dream, but causes the person to forget about the dream, He essentially seals the dream until the time of its fulfillment. It is designed to protect the person in many ways. That is one of the reasons why sometimes people find themselves in a situation and it feels like déjà vu. The familiar feeling is because the Lord had shared the revelation with the person but then sealed it. On the contrary, the thief, the devil, uses this technique to covertly implant a dangerous payload into a person's life, undetected. Therefore, counteract hidden or forgotten demonic dreams by doing a general renunciation of any demonic dreams, and break the resultant covenants. Or, ask the Lord to inform us of any demonic dreams so we can specifically pray against them. The enemy will continue giving these dreams, but will eventually have to slow down or stop because our prayers are rendering his time and efforts null and void. Unless he wants to waste his time by giving us dreams we will immediately reject, rebuke, and return to the sender, and he will have to stop and consider another strategy.

The enemy has a history of doing absolutely dumb things, such as rebelling against God. Yet, he does have wisdom to plan and execute strategic operations. Unfortunately for him, but a blessing for us, is that no one can outwit or outmatch God. In all diligence, we have to remember that we are fighting against a desperate enemy who is trying to escape an outpouring of God's everlasting wrath. The devil knows he will serve a period of incarceration, receive a temporary parole, and then get incarcerated and tormented for all eternity. That makes him the most dangerous kind of criminal because he has nothing left to lose, and so he is putting everything on the line. In all my years of combat, one of the most dangerous threats was a suicide bomber. The most dangerous type of suicide bomber was the one who willingly strapped on a suicide vest with the aim to die and take as many other people on that one-way trip as possible. The devil is that kind of suicide bomber. Sadly, some suicide bombers did so under duress, such as enemy prisoners or those whose family the enemy had kidnapped. Similarly, many workers of iniquity are in serious bondage to the enemy. That is one of the reasons why Jesus told us to bless our human enemies instead of cursing them. Their actions have already brought curses upon themselves, and their families. Even if they are willingly working with the enemy, and enjoying their evil deeds, they are in bondage to the devil. Their prayers may very well end up being their saving grace.

Some people may find it very difficult to pray for people who are persecuting them. However, never forget how Jesus instructed us to handle such situations:

> *'Ye have heard that it hath been said, 'Thou shalt love thy neighbour, and hate thine enemy.' But I say unto you,* **'Love your enemies, bless them that curse you, do good to them that hate you, and pray for them which despitefully use you, and persecute you;** *That ye may be the children of your Father which is in heaven: for He maketh His sun to rise on the evil and on the good, and sendeth rain on the just and on the unjust. For if ye love them which love you, what reward have ye? Do not even the publicans the same? And if ye salute your brethren only, what do ye more than others? Do not even the publicans so? Be ye therefore perfect, even as your Father which is in heaven is perfect.'* ~ Matthew 5:43-48

The devil's strategy includes allowing a person to serve as his representative, with the hopes that we will hate the person until bitterness takes root in our life. That in turn creates space for the devil room to operate. I prayed for everyone who was projecting witchcraft towards me, especially for their children and grandchildren. Such intercessory prayers are easy when we know the potential consequences that witchcraft has on families. Again, based on everything I have experienced, I do not wish anyone to go to hell. Yet, I understand why the Lord directed the Israelites to put witches and false prophets to death. Many people, including workers of iniquity, do not realize just how much they are living by God's grace. Even though I could put a witch or a false prophet to death under the Law of God, I also willingly extend God's grace to them. I have not forgotten that Jesus shed His blood for everyone, and I am grateful that He redeemed me. Tragically, for those workers of iniquity who refuse to except God's grace, on the date of their judgment, the Lord will show them the person, or persons, whom they were persecuting, praying for their salvation. Praying for our enemies is a good thing if our enemies repent. On the contrary, praying for our enemies becomes a part of their damnation because the Lord can say He did everything possible to try to save that individual but the person rejected Him and His grace.

The devil tries to make us forget our dreams, and he will also try to make us forget whom the real enemy is. Consequently, be careful about wrestling with flesh and blood instead of with evil spirits. Likewise, do not wrestle with God and lose sight of the real enemy, the old serpent we call the devil.

Skill To Interpret Demonic Dreams

While I do not invest a lot of time trying to fully interpret a demonic dream or vision, it is important to know what the enemy is trying to accomplish. It is detrimental to ignore a demonic dream or vision, even if we do not know what it means. It helps to know that it is from the enemy and that we should pray against it. If not, our silence makes us complicit in giving the enemy permission to execute his evil plans in our life. As previously mentioned, I had a demonic dream the night "So, You Want to be a Prophet… ARE YOU CRAZY?" was published. It indicated the enemy was going to try to block its publicity, sale, and steal the royalties. I woke up angry at that thieving devil. I vividly recall having a dream when I was in Kuwait, ignorant of the significance of the dream. I saw several copies of the book "Minister to the People" about to go down a drain. Every demonic dream represents forging a covenant with the devil. Knowing what the intended covenant is helps to make us an effective spiritual sniper against the enemy's plans, to include the spirits he releases against us (family, business, ministry, etc.).

I am intimately familiar with the physical and psychological impacts of a potential suicide bomber versus a potential shooter/sniper threat. In the case of a sniper, no one may recognize the threat until a person suddenly gets shot, or, the shooter/sniper misses and the round makes an impact. One of the most effective countermeasures against an enemy sniper is having a sniper on your team. A sniper can effectively identify potential firing points the enemy sniper is using. After all, the friendly sniper would have potentially used those locations based on clear fields of fire, cover and concealment, wind conditions and other factors that impact a sniper's accuracy and efficiency. Another skill for snipers is to call for direct or indirect fire such air support or artillery. A spiritual sniper needs to have a relationship with the Lord and know how to petition Him for resources to spoil the enemy's plans.

To date, the most popular video on the Social Aloe Ministries YouTube channel is about identifying the signs and symptoms of being under a witchcraft attack. Some of those attacks come through dreams and among the most sinister, involves eating. If that sounds farfetched, please examine this Scriptural reference from what we call "The Last Supper":

> "Jesus answered, *'He it is, to whom I shall give a sop, when I have dipped it.'* And when He had dipped the sop, He gave it to Judas Iscariot, the son of Simon. **And after the sop Satan entered into him.** Then said Jesus unto him, *'That thou doest, do quickly.'"* ~ John 13:26-28

I had two dreams; the first involved a graphic scene where I saw someone carving a dog like a turkey. I prayed against it and fell asleep and had a second dream, where I was eating a strip of bacon. Shockingly, the "bacon" looked like it came from the dead dog in the previous dream, and even worse, it was not fully cooked.

THE PROCESS: THE REFINER'S FIRE

This book would be much larger if I had presented all of the sinister attacks I even bothered to record. There was a time when I felt like writing the demonic dreams and visions that may have been fueling the devil, so I stopped. Well, I stopped but he did not. One of the first things that came to mind after that dream was how someone was going to hell for these attacks against me, and the ministry to which the Lord has called me. Then I fasted and prayed against that dream. Now, while that combination of dreams was clearly absolutely wicked, I had some that were not. I had a dream where someone was offering me cookies and candy, to include some peanut M&M's. Whatsoever the enemy was trying to feed me, which may have been worse than the dead dog, it was giftwrapped to trap. Those dreams, and the numerous others that people will have to stand before the Lord and give an account for, are perversions of when the Lord fed Ezekiel and John:

> "Moreover He said unto me, *'Son of man, eat that thou findest; eat this roll, and go speak unto the house of Israel.'*
>
> So I opened my mouth, and he caused me to eat that roll.
>
> And He said unto me, *'Son of man, cause thy belly to eat, and fill thy bowels with this roll that I give thee.'*
>
> Then did I eat it; and it was in my mouth as honey for sweetness.
>
> And He said unto me, *'Son of man, go, get thee unto the house of Israel, and speak with My Words unto them.'"* ~ Ezekiel 3:1-4
>
> "And the voice which I heard from heaven spake unto me again, and said, *'Go and take the little book which is open in the hand of the angel which standeth upon the sea and upon the earth.'*
>
> And I went unto the angel, and said unto him, *'Give me the little book.'*
>
> And he said unto me, *'Take it, and eat it up; and it shall make thy belly bitter, but it shall be in thy mouth sweet as honey.'*
>
> And I took the little book out of the angel's hand, and ate it up; and it was in my mouth sweet as honey: and as soon as I had eaten it, my belly was bitter.

> And he said unto me, *'Thou must prophesy again before many peoples, and nations, and tongues, and kings.'"* ~ Revelation 10:8-11

There was also an obviously sinister dream where a spirit came to me in the form of someone I know. The vision lasted a few seconds, but it had a storyline like the person had been cooking downstairs and brought some food to my bedroom for me to try. There was a momentary daze as I wondered why the person was in my house. Then the spirit, masquerading as the friend, offered me a sample. My refusal was not enough because the masquerading spirit then tried forcing the "food" into my mouth.

Hypocrisy

The unrighteous try to hold the righteous to the standards of the Lord they fail to meet themselves. While that is a form of hypocrisy, the Lord uses the kingdom of darkness at times to fulfill His agenda. There is a tendency to forget that the devil is not free to do as he pleases. Even though iniquity was found in him, and he became rebellious, it does not mean he is not subject to the Lord's dominion. As the saying goes, satan is the devil but he is God's devil. The following exemplifies that:

> And the devil, taking Him up into an high mountain, shewed unto Him all the kingdoms of the world in a moment of time. And the devil said unto Him, *'All this power will I give Thee, and the glory of them: for that is delivered unto me; and to whomsoever I will I give it. If Thou therefore wilt worship me, all shall be Thine.'*
>
> And Jesus answered and said unto him, *'Get thee behind Me, satan: for it is written, 'Thou shalt **worship the Lord thy God, and Him only shalt thou serve.**'"* ~ Luke 4:5-8

In shutting down the devil's attempts to lead Jesus into sin by obeying him, Jesus reminded the devil of his place because the Lord was still the devil's God. When Jesus ascended back into heaven, there are several Scriptures, to include 1 Peter 3:21-2, which remind us that Jesus has all power and authority over everyone. The devil is subject unto Christ Jesus. I like how the Holy Spirit inspired this insightful explanation: "Thou hast put all things in subjection under His feet. For in that He put all in subjection under Him, He left nothing that is not put under Him. But now we see not yet all things put under Him." ~ Hebrews 2:8 As a result, in many ways, the devil is Jesus's devil, and even when the devil is working against the Lord he may be unknowingly working for the Lord. A great example of this is how the devil's afflictions may be a sign of damnation that is actually meant to lead to a person's salvation:

> "It is reported commonly that there is fornication among you, and such fornication as is not so much as named among the Gentiles, that one should have his father's wife. And ye are puffed up, and have not rather mourned, that he that hath done this deed might be taken away from among you. For I verily, as absent in body, but present in spirit, have judged already, as though I were present, concerning him that hath so done this deed, In the name of our Lord Jesus Christ, when ye are gathered together, and my spirit, with the power of our Lord Jesus Christ, To **deliver such an one unto satan for the destruction of the flesh, that the spirit may be saved in the day of the Lord Jesus.** Your glorying is not good. **Know ye not that a little leaven leaveneth the whole lump? Purge out therefore the old leaven, that ye may be a new lump, as ye are unleavened.** For even Christ our Passover is sacrificed for us: Therefore let us keep the feast, not with old leaven, neither with the leaven of malice and wickedness; but with the unleavened bread of sincerity and truth." ~ 1 Corinthians 5:1-8

The Lord sometimes uses the devil to purge the leaven from a person. Especially because of my calling, I cannot afford to be a hypocrite. Therefore, my desire for deliverance from these devils is more about gaining freedom from sin instead of simply freedom from the consequences of sin.

Christians, and especially ministers of Christ Jesus, need to keep many things in mind. Among them is the very important task of guarding against hypocrisy, which Jesus described as the leaven of the Pharisees (Luke 12:1). We should never forget the importance of the following lessons.

> "An instructor of the foolish, a teacher of babes, which hast the form of knowledge and of the truth in the law. Thou therefore which teachest another, teachest thou not thyself? Thou that preachest a man should not steal, dost thou steal? Thou that sayest

a man should not commit adultery, dost thou commit adultery? Thou that abhorrest idols, dost thou commit sacrilege?" ~ Romans 2:20-22

In addition to not doing those things in order to set a good example by honoring Christ Jesus, especially for ministers, we have to give serious consideration to the following warning: "My brethren, be not many masters, knowing that we shall receive the greater condemnation." ~ James 3:1

I can now reveal to others the sins I used to engage in, as a testament of God's grace and holiness. I am also painfully aware of the potential consequences of sin, even on this side of hell. Outwardly, I may look like a hypocrite to some, but inwardly, I am a changed man, one who no longer has a beam in his eye, which means I get to point out even a speck in someone else's eye (Matthew 7:1-5). In fact, I may be able to identify even a speck in someone eye because I once had the same speck that I looked at for years, until the Lord cleansed me with the blood of the Lamb. Let me take the time to add the following very important reminders:

> "If we say that we have fellowship with Him, and walk in darkness, we lie, and do not the truth: But if we walk in the Light, as He is in the Light, we have fellowship one with another, and **the blood of Jesus Christ His Son cleanseth us from ALL sin**. If we say that we have no sin, we deceive ourselves, and the truth is not in us. **If we confess our sins, He is faithful and just to forgive us our sins, and to cleanse us from all unrighteousness.** If we say that we have not sinned, we make Him a liar, and His Word is not in us." ~ 1 John 1:6-10

> "Wherefore henceforth know we no man after the flesh: yea, though we have known Christ after the flesh, yet now henceforth know we Him no more. **Therefore if any man be in Christ, He is a new creature: old things are passed away; behold, all things are become new.** And all things are of God, who hath reconciled us to Himself by Jesus Christ, and hath given to us the ministry of reconciliation; To wit, that God was in Christ, reconciling the world unto Himself, not imputing their trespasses unto them; and hath committed unto us the word of reconciliation.

Now then we are ambassadors for Christ, as though God did beseech you by us: we pray you in Christ's stead, be ye reconciled to God. **For He hath made Him to be sin for us, who knew no sin; that we might be made the righteousness of God in Him.**" ~ 2 Corinthians 5:16-21

"**Christ hath redeemed us** from the curse of the Law, being made a curse for us: for it is written, *'Cursed is every one that hangeth on a tree'*: That the blessing of Abraham might come on the Gentiles through Jesus Christ; that we might receive the promise of the Spirit through faith." ~ Galatians 3:13-14

We know the Lord allowed the devil to afflict Job because he was a righteous man, who loved the Lord, regardless of how much or how little he had. On the first day of Job's tribulation, after losing so much, to include his ten children, this was Job's (initial reaction) reaction:

"Then Job arose, and rent his mantle, and shaved his head, and fell down upon the ground, and worshipped, and said, *'Naked came I out of my mother's womb, and naked shall I return thither: the Lord gave, and the Lord hath taken away; blessed be the name of the Lord.'*" ~ Job 1:20-21

I say initial reaction because some people make it seem as if a person will remain upbeat during every moment of a tribulation. Arguably, if you can go through a tribulation without experiencing some form of frustration and/or outburst, you are either very gifted or that is not a true tribulation. Lest not forget the Job later said:

"After this opened Job his mouth, and cursed his day. And Job spake, and said, *'Let the day perish wherein I was born, and the night in which it was said, 'There is a man child conceived.' Let that day be darkness; let not God regard it from above, neither let the light shine upon it. Let darkness and the shadow of death stain it; let a cloud dwell upon it; let the blackness of the day terrify it. As for that night, let darkness seize upon it; let it not be joined unto the days of the year, let it not come into the number of the months. Lo, let that night be solitary, let no joyful voice come therein. Let them curse it that curse the day, who are ready to raise up their mourning. Let the stars of the twilight thereof be dark; let it look for light, but have none; neither let it see the dawning of the day: Because it shut not up the doors of my mother's womb, nor hid sorrow from mine eyes.*

Why died I not from the womb? Why did I not give up the ghost when I came out of the belly? Why did the knees prevent me? Or why the breasts that I should suck? For now should I have lain still and been quiet, I should have slept: then had I been at rest, With kings and counsellors of the earth, which build desolate places for themselves; Or with princes that had gold, who filled their houses with silver: Or as an hidden untimely birth I had not been; as infants which never saw light. There the wicked cease from troubling; and there the weary be at rest. There the prisoners rest together; they hear not the voice of the oppressor. The small and great are there; and the servant is free from his master.

Wherefore is light given to him that is in misery, and life unto the bitter in soul; Which long for death, but it cometh not; and dig for it more than for hid treasures; Which rejoice exceedingly, and are glad, when they can find the grave? Why is light given to a man whose way is hid, and whom God hath hedged in? For my sighing cometh before I eat, and my roarings are poured out like the waters. For the thing which I greatly feared is come upon me, and that which I was afraid of is come unto me. I was not in safety, neither had I rest, neither was I quiet; yet trouble came." ~ Job 3:1-26

In my opinion, being pushed to or near to one's breaking point is a hallmark of a tribulation. Some people have gone through a tribulation where they cursed the Lord and quit, which is what the devil wants people to do, especially to make them quit serving and loving the Lord. Too many people sanitize their struggles to make it seem as if they were not pushed to the point of hating life, possibly regretting they had been born or simply asked the Lord to kill them. I asked the Lord to kill me a few times, and as of today's date, I do not regret any of those requests because I seriously wanted to die. I will not pretend as if things did not get that bad. There were even times when I did not want anyone to try to tell me that God loved me, or, that He wanted to deliver me. It is not comforting when people claim the Lord wants to do something, which is why we have been crying out to Him, but no one can tell us why He has not done anything, or, since He wants to, when He will bring some relief.

Whereas Job's afflictions were due to his righteousness, demonic oppression is a consequence of rebelling against the Lord. In Job's case however, the Lord lifted His hedge of protection so the devil could afflict Job. Likewise, the Lord can lift His hedge of protection from around us, leaving us more vulnerable to the enemy's attacks. In some cases, the Lord lifts His hedge of protection and sends a devil to afflict us. If that sounds like a side of the Lord you have never heard of, let me expose you to the God of the Bible. As I convey these words, my trial required some "soul-searching" to ensure rebellion was not at the core of why I was suffering. One of the enemy's techniques is to make a person feel as if a trial means he or she is at enmity with the Lord. While that is sometimes the case, a trial may simply be a tool the Lord uses to refine us, possibly in preparation for a promotion. For example, the Lord said, *'Behold, I have refined thee, but not with silver; I have chosen thee in the furnace of affliction. For Mine own sake, even for Mine own sake, will I do it: for how should My name be polluted? And I will not give My glory unto another.'* ~ Isaiah 48:10-11

Sadly, some people who are at enmity with God cannot even begin to imagine that being the case. They may cry about being persecuted when the Lord is actually prosecuting them. They are so deceived and/or arrogant that they cannot even begin to fathom that the Lord is the source of their dilemma. Therefore, prosecution is dubbed as persecution. For example, King Saul suffered demonic oppression because of his rebellion against the Lord. The devil tried convincing me that my tribulation, and the open door why he would not leave, was because I was rebelling against the Lord by not marrying a certain person. Such a thing may sound plausible, which is how the devil works. The devil could even use the events in Jonah 1-2 to make a potentially convincing case. After all, Jonah rebelled against the Lord so He sent a storm after him, one that threatened to break up the ship Jonah was on. Consequently, the sailors threw Jonah overboard, which was how he ended up in the belly of the whale. That was when Jonah cried out to the Lord, and He then gave the prophet a second chance to do what He had initially directed Jonah to do. It demonstrates how we have freewill but the Lord controls the circumstance that can impact our decisions. In the case of prophets, they operate under "divine constraint". A prophet of the Lord does not have the free will of other Christians, hence the process. We see this when the Lord said to Jeremiah: *'Say not, I am a child: for thou shalt go to all that I shall send thee, and whatsoever I command thee thou shalt speak… Thou therefore gird up thy loins, and arise, and speak unto them all that I command thee: be not dismayed at their faces, lest I confound thee before them.'* ~ Jeremiah 1:7, 17

A person who is battling demonic oppression truly needs to hear from the Lord regarding what is going on and why. Any form of intelligence from the enemy is usually counterintelligence, which is a part of his psychological warfare. The devil's job is to keep us in bondage instead of helping us to get out of it. And he certainly has no limits to what he will do to ensnare us, to include trying to get us to marry the wrong person. You may have heard that the teacher is silent during the test. Well, the Lord is sometimes silent on the crucial information we are most interested in. He may communicate many things to us, to include how to get others out of their bondage, while leaving us in the dark. It may seem cruel at times, but the Lord is using the afflictions to prepare us for greater levels of service to and relationship with Him. When travelling in the dark, remember, what the Lord said to the disenchanted prophet who petitioned the Lord by asking, *'O Lord, how long shall I cry, and Thou wilt not hear! Even cry out unto Thee of violence, and Thou wilt not save!'* ~ Habakkuk 1:2. The Lord's response included, *'...**the just shall live by his faith.**'* ~ Habakkuk 2:4b.

I also wondered when the Lord was going to deliver me from this evil. I absolutely hated having a devil living in my house, especially one that was so bold. Yet, each passing day meant that devil had less time to do what it had been allowed to do. For the most part, one of my best courses of action was to sharpen the sword I was going to use to cut that devil asunder when given the chance. So no, this was not a tribulation because I had refused to marry someone the Lord wanted me to marry. The only ones who were presenting such an argument were the devil and his emissaries. If the Lord really wanted me to marry someone I was not attracted to, He could have turned my heart towards that person. Some love stories started off with both people not liking each other, or, one person not liking the other, but things changed either based on their interactions or the Lord turning hearts. If you do not believe the Lord changes people's hearts, here is some of what the Bible says about that matter:

- "**And the Lord hardened the heart of pharaoh**, and he hearkened not unto them; as the Lord had spoken unto Moses." ~ Exodus 9:12
- *'And I will give them one heart, and I will put a new spirit within you; and **I will take the stony heart out of their flesh, and will give them an heart of flesh:** That they may walk in My statutes, and keep Mine

- *ordinances, and do them: and they shall be My people, and I will be their God.'* ~ Ezekiel 11:19-20
- "And it was so, that when he [Saul] had turned his back to go from Samuel, **God gave him another heart**: and all those signs came to pass that day." ~ 1 Samuel 10:9

I said the Lord might send a devil to afflict a person. That may seem blasphemous to some people, but before you start stoning me, it is written:

> "Then Samuel took the horn of oil, and anointed him in the midst of his brethren: and the Spirit of the Lord came upon David from that day forward. So Samuel rose up, and went to Ramah.
>
> **But the Spirit of the Lord departed from Saul, and an evil spirit from the Lord troubled him.**
>
> And Saul's servants said unto him, *'Behold now, an evil spirit from God troubleth thee. Let our lord now command thy servants, which are before thee, to seek out a man, who is a cunning player on an harp: and it shall come to pass, when the evil spirit from God is upon thee, that he shall play with his hand, and thou shalt be well.'*
>
> And Saul said unto his servants, *'Provide me now a man that can play well, and bring him to me.'*
>
> Then answered one of the servants, and said, *'Behold, I have seen a son of Jesse the Bethlehemite, that is cunning in playing, and a mighty valiant man, and a man of war, and prudent in matters, and a comely person, and the Lord is with him.'*
>
> Wherefore Saul sent messengers unto Jesse, and said, *'Send me David thy son, which is with the sheep.'*
>
> And Jesse took an ass laden with bread, and a bottle of wine, and a kid, and sent them by David his son unto Saul.
>
> And David came to Saul, and stood before him: and he loved him greatly; and he became his armourbearer. And Saul sent to Jesse, saying, *'Let David, I pray thee, stand before me; for he hath found favour in my sight.'*

And it came to pass, **when the evil spirit from God was upon Saul**, that David took an harp, and played with his hand: so Saul was refreshed, and was well, and the evil spirit departed from him." ~ 1 Samuel 16:13-23

In addition to Samuel having told Saul that the Lord had rejected him as king, and was seeking His replacement, a clear indication of why an evil spirit was afflicting him, was when Saul's men confirmed where the evil spirit had come from. Another example of the Lord sending an evil spirit to afflict a person or group of individuals is found in Judges 9:22-24, which states:

"When Abimelech had reigned three years over Israel, Then **God sent an evil spirit between Abimelech and the men of Shechem**; and the men of Shechem dealt treacherously with Abimelech: That the cruelty done to the threescore and ten sons of Jerubbaal might come, and their blood be laid upon Abimelech their brother, which slew them; and upon the men of Shechem, which aided him in the killing of his brethren."

Ministers who blaspheme and/or use the Lord's name in vain need to study 1 Kings 22, with the 400 false prophets left in king Ahab's court. The prophets were liars to begin with, plus Ahab was not interested in hearing the truth. Therefore, as a part of Ahab's judgment, and that of the false prophets, the prophet Micaiah, a prophet of the Lord, clearly said, *'Now therefore, behold,* **the Lord hath put a lying spirit in the mouth of all these thy prophets,** *and the Lord hath spoken evil concerning thee.'* ~ 1 Kings 22:23. If you still do not believe your spiritual woes may be because the Lord sent an impure spirit to refine you, or worse, as a part of your judgment or someone you are ministering to, I present this final exhibit:

'And if the prophet be deceived when he hath spoken a thing, **I the Lord have deceived that prophet,** *and I will stretch out My hand upon him, and will destroy him from the midst of My people Israel. And they shall bear the punishment of their iniquity: the punishment of the prophet shall be even as the punishment of him that seeketh unto him.'* ~ Ezekiel 14:9-10

THE PROCESS: THE REFINER'S FIRE

Obey God: People Lie, God Does Not

I learned a hard lesson the hard way when comes to obeying God. Many people say the Holy Spirit is a gentleman, as if He is soft. Quite frankly, too many people treat the Holy Spirit as if He is not God. Have you ever heard people ministering, healing for example, and they keep saying, "More Lord" as if the Lord does not know how to heal a person and He requires a human to guide Him. We typically view the Holy Spirit as the small still voice of the Lord, while forgetting that when the day of Pentecost had come, the Holy Spirit descended on the earth as a rushing mighty wind (1 Kings 19:12-13, Acts 2:1-2). Lest not forget the Holy Spirit killed Ananias and Sapphira for lying to Him (Acts 5:1-11).

Now that I have reintroduced or introduced you to the Holy Spirit, Jesus said one of the Holy Spirit's functions was to show us things to come. To make a long story short, I drove the (false) prophetess and her armor bearer to Sikeston, Missouri for her ordination ceremony. We checked into hotel. They shared a room on the first floor, in part because of the armor bearer's disabilities, which was a part of why I ended up being a gentleman and agreed to take them on the 600-mile one-way drive. One of the mistakes I made was to not consult with the Lord prior to the trip. However, that paled in comparison to what happened next. I was unpacking and getting settled in when I heard, "Get in your car and leave." I was not as far along with testing the spirit as I am now. When I heard that, I disobeyed the Lord by rationalizing He would not wait until I got 600 miles away from home to give me such a message to leave two ladies stranded. Well, they could have gotten a ride home that would have slightly inconvenienced someone else. The timing was not the best for me, but at least it was before I came under demonic attack a few times the following day, Halloween, the day when witchcraft is at its peak around the world. The first attack was while we were praying the false prophetess at her ordination ceremony. But that paled in comparison that night when the false prophecy was released about the Lord wanted me to marry her. My life would have been easier if I had obeyed the Lord, gotten in my car and left.

I also learned to trust my personal relationship with the Lord more than anyone else's relationship with Him, regardless of their title. Many people do not hear from the Lord as well or as much as they used to because they have allowed someone to serve as their intermediary. It is similar to how the Israelites said they did not want to hear from the Lord directly and He should speak to Moses who would relay the messages to them (Exodus 20:19). That is why some people get manipulated into thinking they have to go to church so the pastor can give them the Word of the Lord. Hence, many people have been spiritually castrated and are now like spiritual eunuchs. If someone needs ministry, they know how to call the pastor for help even though they may be more gifted than him in that aspect. They have surrendered their gifts and calling from the Lord to a pastor. Therefore, they call on the pastor when in some cases the pastor should be calling on them. Personal and ministerial growth always get stifled under the wrong leadership. We have to remember that those who are led by the Spirit of God are the sons of God (Romans 8:14). Above all, we have to let the Holy Spirit lead us, to include whether we should be a part of a church or not, and also which church to attend. I had a dream where I was in a church with a pastor who was leading people dressed as Mennonites. Then, suddenly, I saw people dressed in whimsical outfits, looking like fairies, filing into the church. The Lord was letting me know the pastor was a witch, giving the appearance of being holy. We really need a deep personal relationship with the Lord. On the day of Jesus's crucifixion, one of the monumental events was the tearing of the veil that covered the holy of holies. We need to ensure we do not try to repair that veil. We need to boldly approach the throne of grace, which is a part of our heritage in Christ Jesus (Hebrews 4:16).

Love Triangle: Why The Devil Fought Harder For Me

Jesus said no one could pluck any of His sheep (children) out His hand or His Father's hand (John 10:28-30). But that does not mean the devil will not try. The devil may also try to convince us that he has somehow managed to pluck us out of God's hand, or, that the Lord cannot pluck us out of his hands. There were times when I felt like I was caught in a "love triangle", with two jealous lovers contending over me. This mirrored when Jesus said, *'No man can serve two masters: for either he will hate the one, and love the other; or else he will hold to the one, and despise the other. Ye cannot serve God and mammon.'* ~ Matthew 6:24. The more I loved God was the more I hated the devil. The tighter I held on to the Lord was the harder the devil tried plucking me out of His hand, so I had to get closer to the Lord. Likewise, the harder the devil tried to shut me up, especially from proclaiming the Word of the Lord, was the more I went to the Lord and said, "Use me."

The (spiritual) marital covenant that the evil spirit was trying to get me into was ungodly for many reasons, to include:

- "…Have no fellowship with the unfruitful works of darkness, but rather reprove them." ~ Ephesians 5:11
- "Be ye not unequally yoked together with unbelievers: for what fellowship hath righteousness with unrighteousness? And what communion hath light with darkness? And what concord hath Christ with Belial? Or what part hath he that believeth with an infidel? And what agreement hath the temple of God with idols? For ye are the temple of the living God; as God hath said, *'I will dwell in them, and walk in them; and I will be their God, and they shall be My people. Wherefore come out from among them, and be ye separate'*, saith the Lord, *'and **touch not the unclean thing**; and I will receive you. And will be a Father unto you, and ye shall be My sons and daughters'*, saith the Lord Almighty." ~ 2 Corinthians 6:14-18.
- Marriage, or as I prefer to call it, holy matrimony, is between a man and a woman. Any variant is an abomination unto the Lord, to include a "marriage" between a human and a spirit. Jesus clearly said, *'But from the beginning of the creation God made them male and female. For this cause shall a man leave his father and mother, and cleave to his wife; And they twain shall be one flesh: so then they are no more twain, but one flesh. What therefore God hath joined together, let not man put asunder.'* ~ Mark 10:6-9. While married couples do form deep intimate bonds, sometimes seemingly down to the spiritual level, Jesus said they became *'one flesh'* instead of one spirit. How can a person become *'one flesh'* with a spirit does not have a flesh?
- Jesus shed Light on the legalities of a marriage between two spirits. It is a part of why a spiritual marriage, with the exception of Christ and His bride, which is a nonsexual relationship, is absolutely illegal. Consequently, a devil has to get your consent, whether through ignorance or arrogance, to enter into or stay in such an ungodly union. Jesus said, *'**For in the resurrection they neither marry, nor are given in marriage, but are as the angels of God in heaven.**'* ~ Matthew 22:30. Divorce that devil! God hates

divorce, but not when it comes to divorcing the devil. The Lord wants us to keep our vows (covenants), but not the ones we made with or to the devil. You can sell your soul to the devil but the blood of Christ Jesus can redeem you.

- "And it came to pass, when men began to multiply on the face of the earth, and daughters were born unto them, That the sons of God [angels] saw the daughters of men that they were fair; and they took them wives of all which they chose. And the Lord said, *'My spirit shall not always strive with man, for that he also is flesh: yet his days shall be an hundred and twenty years.'* There were giants in the earth in those days; and also after that, when **the sons of God came in unto the daughters of men, and they bare children to them**, the same became mighty men which were of old, men of renown. And God saw that the wickedness of man was great in the earth, and that every imagination of the thoughts of his heart was only evil continually. And it repented the Lord that He had made man on the earth, and it grieved Him at His heart. And the Lord said, *'I will destroy man whom I have created from the face of the earth; both man, and beast, and the creeping thing, and the fowls of the air; for it repenteth Me that I have made them."* ~ Genesis 6:1-7. Do not let anyone lead you into ungodly covenants, which may very well result in you incurring God's wrath. The devils are already condemned and they are trying to get you to join them too.

- *'Thou shalt have no other gods before Me.'* ~ Exodus 20:3

I could have simply quoted two to three Scriptures. However, I am like a spiritual machine gun when it comes to the enemy. I have a function switch that goes from "Safe" to "Automatic". Whenever the enemy messes with me, I send a barrage of fire back his way. I do not fire warning shots at the enemy, everything is meant to inflict maximum casualties, while ensuring nothing raises its ugly head again. If you were to spend a year of your life, trying to get rid of a devil that does its best to torment you, such as the noises it is making upstairs as I type at this very moment, you would have zero tolerance for certain things. Hate is not a strong enough word to describe what I feel for these devils after this journey. By the way, the above Scriptures are great for praying against an ungodly spiritual marriage.

The wannabe "spiritual spouse" was like Phaltiel, following behind and lamenting over the loss of his beloved Michal to king David. As emotionally riveting as it may have been to all who were present, it was not going to make an ounce of difference. He was in an ungodly covenant with someone he could never have because she belonged to someone else, the king. Likewise, I belonged to Christ Jesus, the King of kings and the Lord of lords, the one who paid the price for all of me. In addition, I wanted Jesus and Him alone. I hated that devil for how it was trying to ruin my life, to include my relationship with Christ, and I literally wanted to kill it. Like that foul spirit, Phaltiel tried holding on to Michal, until Abner told him to go home. Whereas Abner only told Phaltiel once for him to relent, the spirit trying to be my spouse required a persistent shower of rejection for it to relent. Yet, it still wanted to hang around, as if it were my safety net, just in case my relationship with the Lord did not work out, which is laughable. I reject and rebuke that foul spirit.

I often wondered where my "Abner" was, the emissary of the Lord who would tell this spirit to leave, once and for all, because it knew disobeying that command meant it would pay a price much greater than it could bear. I wondered if my deliverance would come through an emissary or if Jesus would show up Himself. My personal choice is the latter. While the reasons are many, one is simply after all this posturing, all this disrespect towards the Lord of lords and King of kings, I would really like to see how brave, big, bad, and mighty the spirit is in front of Jesus. I also deliberated why Jesus said, *'Behold, I give unto you power to tread on serpents and scorpions, and over all the power of the enemy: and nothing shall by any means hurt you.'* ~ Luke 10:19. Yet, despite those Words, so many people failed to permanently get rid of the devil. Also, a burning question is why the devil would not obey my commands to leave. It was literally like a former romantic interest, to include a former spouse, who refuses to accept the fact that the relationship is over.

Remarkably, the spirit's stubborn refusal to give up on me, and let me go, mirrored the witch's stubbornness. Both of them knew I did not love them, and more importantly, I never would love them, yet that did not seem to matter to them at all. It even appeared as if they wanted to be with me so they could say I belong to them, ruin my future, steal my joy, sabotage my life, destroy my ministry, and get pleasure from making me absolutely miserable. Yet, they consider themselves "wife material" and are very bossy about it. Maybe they could be wives to someone, but neither qualifies to be my wife. I am not sexually, emotionally, mentally, or spiritually attracted to either of them. There is no fellowship between light and darkness. I almost forgot about one of their most sinister assignments, which was to keep me away from the woman the Lord had actually ordained for me. It is absolutely demonic to pursue a relationship with someone who clearly does not want you. It is worse if a part of your agenda is to prevent that person from being with someone the Lord intended him or her to be with. **Please, have little to nothing to do with someone who absolutely cannot stand to see you happy, not even for a minute, yet wants to be in a relationship with you.** By the way, Phaltiel cried because of Michal's departure but we do not know if she lamented over being removed from him and returned to David. I wonder if she grown attached to him, or even fallen in love with him? Well, I can attest, I have no love for the masquerading familiar spirit that ruined my life for so many years. It was like an employee who stole a company's money, and even ran customers off, yet wanted the "employee of the month" title. I do not reward bad behavior.

There were times when I wondered why it seemed as if the devil was fighting harder for me but the Lord was not fighting at all. That changed one night in my office when the Lord directed me to get a rubber band from the drawer on the right side of my desk. I retrieved a rubber band and the Lord directed me to hold on to it with two fingers from one hand. Once secured, He directed me to pull on it with the other hand and then let it go. I obeyed and pulled the rubber band a few inches and then let it go. I did it a few times, which stung every time I released the rubber band. It was a "Jeremiah 18 Moment" because the Lord used a natural example to illustrate the supernatural truth that He actually had me, securely in His hand. The devil was fighting harder for me because he does not have me. In accordance with James 4:7, and Job 1-2, the devil can only pull me so far, before letting go because as long as I hold on to the Lord, and more importantly, He will keep holding on to me. The enemy was also trying to stretch me to my breaking point. However, even if I were to break, I would still remain in the Lord's hand. Also of note was the sting I felt upon releasing the rubber band. Not that I care, but it "hurts" the devil to let me go, in part because that loser, who has already lost, hates losing to his

Creator and Master. Again, the devil is the Lord's devil and the devil is eternally subject to Christ Jesus. Then there is the other side of the hurt, which many seldom consider when going through a tribulation.

While trials help to conform us into the image of Christ Jesus, it does not mean the Lord gets pleasure from seeing us suffer or that He does not feel the sting of our sufferings. Lazarus when through a trial for the glorification of God, but Jesus wept (John 11:35). When Shadrach, Meshach, and Abednego were in king Nebuchadnezzar's fire, there appeared one in the fire who looked like the Son of God (Daniel 3). The Christophany was a preincarnate appearance of Jesus, in the fire when those men. We usually feel as if the Lord is distant from us during dark periods. However, Jesus is that friend who sticks to us "...closer than a brother" (Proverbs 18:24b). By the way, the three men emerging from the fire without even smelling like smoke is reminiscent of a promise from the Lord to me. Hence the painting on the cover of "On Trial: A Test of My Faith". The fire would refine and strengthen my faith in the Lord but it would not destroy me. I went through things that could have sent me to a mental asylum. It is purely by God's grace that I survived, in great physical, mental, emotional, and spiritual health. Such was the case with Paul who had a messenger of satan afflicting him, but God's grace was sufficient for him (2 Corinthians 12:7-10). That same grace is sufficient for me too.

The devil was fighting harder for me because he did not have me, Jesus did. Anyone who rebels against the Lord is wasting precious time and energy trying to usurp His authority. Jesus did not have to fight for whom He already had; He simply and calmly kept holding on to me. In a similar vein, do not misconstrue a person's efforts to be or stay with you, or jealousy over you, as a sign of love. Some jealousy is not based on love. In many cases, jealousy is in fact love's destructive counterpart, which is based on insecurity and possessiveness. In the case of the witch, she contended over me with an ungodly jealousy, even ignoring the fact that I was not attracted to her in any way. As a point of discussion, what would she have gained from capturing someone who did not, could not, and would not love her? There is no spell or sorcery that powerful. Three years of employing the dark arts failed miserably. Consequently, I do not consider it strange that a spirit of homosexuality was sent to me to try to change my sexual preference. It is reminiscent of a case of, "If I cannot have you, no other woman will." More than likely, that spirit would have remained dormant, waited for me to marry one of the Lord's daughters, and then begin trying to destroy the marriage. I hope this testimony encourages you to pray for your future spouse if you are single, or your spouse if you are married. The devil is out to destroy God-ordained marriages.

The covert messenger of satan gave me an appreciation for executing the *'righteous judgment'* Jesus spoke of (John 7:24), which includes the potential spiritual aspects associated with situations. For example, why would a pastor leave his devoted wife of many years for another woman? People may hastily brand him as an adulterer, oblivious to the fact that a witch may have ensnared him, such as what the Lord described in Ezekiel 13:17-23. We also see an example of such a demonic snare when the Lord said:

> *'For among My people are found wicked men: they lay wait, as he that setteth snares;* **they set a trap, they catch men.** *As a cage is full of birds, so are their houses full of deceit: therefore they are become great, and waxen rich. They are waxen fat, they shine: yea, they overpass the deeds of the wicked: they judge not the cause, the cause of the fatherless, yet they prosper; and the right of the needy do they not judge. Shall I not visit for these things?'* saith the Lord: *'shall not My soul be avenged on such a nation as this?'* ~ Jeremiah 5:26-29.

Please, pray for the Lord's ministers. Also, keep in mind that the Lord said, *'…Smite the shepherd, and the sheep shall be scattered: and I will turn mine hand upon the little ones.'* ~ Zechariah 13:7. The devil attacks the shepherds because he is after you, the Lord's sheep. The above Scriptures are vital parts of a spiritual sniper's arsenal against the enemy's snares. While most United States service members are issued weapons that fire a 5.56mm round, some snipers carry sniper rifles that fire a much larger, powerful, and lethal round, to include .50 caliber. The lethality of the latter is greater, with an extended range over the former. In fact, a .50 caliber round is classified as being anti-personnel and anti-equipment because it will disable or destroy some vehicles.

There are times when the Lord showed me the enemy's plans, but He did not allow me to stop them, which was agonizingly frustrating. I wanted to destroy the enemy via prayer from a distance before allowing him to get close enough to do any damage to me. When it comes to spiritual warfare, prayer is an effective long-range weapon that we can use against the enemy. When I was in the military, I did a study of the Battle of Cowpens (South Carolina), on which the movie "The Patriot" was based. There was a time when the American revolutionary forces were told to not fire on the advancing British forces until they could see the whites of their eyes. That is an example of what is called "danger close". The Americans took casualties while waiting for their opportunity to strike back. It takes a tremendous amount of discipline to not retaliate sooner. But, the American commanders had good reasons for issuing such an order in order to accomplish their battle strategies. Moreover, when the Americans could see the whites of the eyes of the British troops, things began to shift, drastically. I was under similar orders from the Lord regarding not going after the witch, regardless of what she did. That was in part because the Lord was going to take care of her by Himself, which is very scary. Lest not forget that Jesus said, *'...fear not them which kill the body, but are not able to kill the soul: but rather fear Him which is able to destroy both soul and body in hell.'* ~ Matthew 10:28. Many people forget about that, and take the Lord too lightly, which is something done at their own peril. "For we know Him that hath said, *'Vengeance belongeth unto Me, I will recompense'*, saith the Lord. And again, *'The Lord shall judge His people.'* **It is a fearful thing to fall into the hands of the living God.**" ~ Hebrews 10:30-31

The trials gave me some practical experiences similar to those of David. The rebellious king Saul pursued David for years in an effort to kill him, and his calling from the Lord. David was extremely disciplined to not retaliate. That was despite the multiple and public attempts on his life at the hands of Saul. He could have killed the rebellious king, at least twice, but David kept his distance and left Saul to the Lord. No one would have blamed David for killing Saul, yet David waited on the Lord to deliver him. I too could have taken the witch's life, at least twice, but like the Lord said about Jezebel, He gave her space to repent (Revelation 2:21). It is a scary thing when the Lord gives a person time to repent but the person squanders the time and opportunities. I know the Lord loves righteousness and judgment (Psalm 33:5). Those traits are also echoed in the following:

> "Depart from evil, and do good; and dwell for evermore. For **the Lord loveth judgment, and forsaketh not His saints; they**

are preserved for ever: but the seed of the wicked shall be cut off. The righteous shall inherit the land, and dwell therein for ever. The mouth of the righteous speaketh wisdom, and his tongue talketh of judgment. The law of his God is in his heart; none of his steps shall slide. The wicked watcheth the righteous, and seeketh to slay him. The Lord will not leave him in his hand, nor condemn him when he is judged. **Wait on the Lord, and keep His way, and He shall exalt thee to inherit the land: when the wicked are cut off, thou shalt see it.** I have seen the wicked in great power, and spreading himself like a green bay tree. Yet he passed away, and, lo, he was not: yea, I sought him, but he could not be found. Mark the perfect man, and behold the upright: for the end of that man is peace. But the transgressors shall be destroyed together: the end of the wicked shall be cut off. But the salvation of the righteous is of the Lord: He is their strength in the time of trouble. And **the Lord shall help them, and deliver them: He shall deliver them from the wicked, and save them, because they trust in Him.**" ~ Psalm 37:27-40

It was frustrating at times being armed and dangerous, and more than willing to dispatch the enemy, but out of obedience to the Lord, I had to stand down and take the beating that came with inaction or delayed action. Please note, as a result of my many sufferings, now I have even fewer inhibitions to "squeezing the trigger" as soon as I see the enemy coming. I have seen what the enemy will do if allowed to get within his striking distance and maximum effective range (for his plans and operations). I have a deep desire to expeditiously stop him dead in his tracks, from a distance. A part of that is because of how long it took for him to get out of my life, and the multiple instances when he trampled on the blood of Christ Jesus. Vengeance is the Lord's, but I want to help destroy the enemy's kingdom for what he did to me and to so many others, especially those who were ignorant of his devices. By releasing a spirit of homosexuality against me was also a part of a sinister plot to attack my salvation. The Bible say even the effeminate shall not inherit the kingdom of heaven (1 Corinthians 6:9-10). The aforementioned rubber band analogy served as an example of why the Holy Spirit is called The Comforter, and how Jesus, The Prince of Peace, gives us peace that transcends human understanding. Jesus is the calm in the storm. On a final note, I was still ministering during this trial, but I would not lay hands on anyone.

Timing

In addition to doing things in accordance with God's will, ways, and Words, we also have to do things in accordance to His timing. There was a time when I was painfully aware that I could not expedite this process, which the Lord knew I would if I could, if He would let me. I still fought because I would not give anything to the devil. Yet, I had to be careful that I was not fighting against the Lord. The life of Jesus gives us a sense of the Lord's timing. The following Scriptures epitomize the importance of the Lord's timing, whether it is time to wait or proceed:

- At the wedding at Cana, Jesus said to Mary, *'Woman, what have I to do with thee? Mine hour is not yet come.'* ~ John 2:4
- "When Jesus therefore perceived that they would come and take Him by force, to make Him a king, He departed again into a mountain Himself alone." ~ John 6:15. It was not time for Jesus' coronation. However, after Jesus' resurrection, things changed, drastically: "Who is gone into heaven, and is on the right hand of God; angels and authorities and powers being made subject unto Him." ~ 1 Peter 3:18-22. In addition, Revelation 20:1-7 speaks of Christ Jesus' thousand year (millennial) reign here on earth.
- "Then cometh He to His disciples, and saith unto them, *'Sleep on now, and take your rest: behold, the hour is at hand, and the Son of man is betrayed into the hands of sinners.'"* ~ Matthew 26:45
- "These Words spake Jesus, and lifted up His eyes to heaven, and said, ***Father, the hour is come;*** *glorify Thy Son, that Thy Son also may glorify Thee: As Thou hast given Him power over all flesh, that He should give eternal life to as many as Thou hast given Him. And this is life eternal, that they might know Thee the only true God, and Jesus Christ, whom Thou hast sent. I have glorified Thee on the earth: I have finished the work which Thou gavest Me to do. And now, O Father, glorify Thou Me with Thine own self with the glory which I had with Thee before the world was."* ~ John 17:1-5

I have seen other ministers, even some who started their ministries after mine, progress ahead of me. No matter how hard I tried, the body of evidence clearly communicated that my hour had not come. When our appointed time with and/or from the Lord comes, no one, not even the devil himself can stop it. I boldly say that in part because of the following:

- God cannot lie (Titus 1:2, Numbers 23:19, 1 Samuel 15:29, etc.)
- His Words do not return to Him void but must accomplish His intent (Isaiah 55:8-11)
- No one can annul His plans (Isaiah 14:27)
- His plans cannot be thwarted (Job 42:2-3)
- There is no God besides God the Father, Jesus His Son, and the Holy Spirit; all three are one (Isaiah 44:6-8, 45:5; 1 John 5:7-8)

I quote a lot of Scriptures because the Sword of the Spirit, which is the Word of God, is most effective against the devil. Therefore, just like Jesus, I use it to block, parry, and thrust the devil through. Because the devil also knows the Word of God, we need to know the Word of God in its proper context, and cling to what the Lord has conveyed to us. The devil will try to have us let go of the truth in favor of his twisted version of the truth, just like he did through the lying Bethelite prophet in 1 Kings 13. One of the many things that helped me through this dreadful process was a refusal to let go of what I knew the Lord revealed to me. I would only let go of promises from the Lord if those things become idols. I willingly sacrificed those things to preserve my relationship with the Lord Jesus, and to give the enemy no room or excuse to operate in my life. If the Lord wants me to have something I know He will give it to me in His own way and timing. Similarly, if He does not want me to have something, He will take it away or prevent me from having it.

Misery Loves Company

Can you imagine being assigned to spend a lot of time with someone you absolutely dislike, but have to pretend to like the person to get closer to him or her? Demons hate us and one of their worst assignments is to spend time with a believer who is fully committed to the Lord Jesus. Demons are an absolutely miserable bunch whose only source of joy is to make others feel miserable, just like them. They are even more miserable because they despise us for having the joy of the Lord, something they had, lost, and will never regain. Praise and worship to the Lord is a weapon during times of affliction. It absolutely blows the minds of devils that we can praise the

Lord while suffering for His name. Devils are miserable, and as the saying goes, "Misery loves company." Armed with this knowledge, despite our afflictions, we should find and maintain our joy with and in the Lord. Devils absolutely love it when we break down to the point of cursing God for our afflictions. Be mindful that the devils are our enemies and the source of our afflictions. Praise the Lord for His goodness, which has the secondary effects of making devils even more miserable. No matter how bad things get, God is still good, and Jesus is still Lord. Never allow your hatred for anything to eclipse your love for the Lord.

Since I lived alone, the enemy thought he had me to himself. Being alone was not a source of misery for me because even when people were around, I have been what some would call a "loaner" for most of my life. I was very content with simply having one good friend. But now, I am never alone because Christ is always with me. My body is a temple of the Holy Spirit, and with His presence, I am never alone, and neither are any of you. A part of why I had to renounce the woman I had been waiting on, and even marriage, was not because I desired to be alone, or, was frustrated with the process and/or the wait. I did it because I did not want to have any idols. I learned the hard way about how the enemy can use the desires of our heart, to include the promises of God, to bring misery into our life. I found so much joy and peace once I let go of those idolatrous things and placed my focus solely on Christ Jesus. I even noticed a decrease in the intensity of the demonic attacks. Please note, more than likely, when we are happy, the enemy is even more miserable. Do not allow the devil to steal your joy.

My years in the wilderness included a lot of isolation and insulation. There were times when I went for a week without seeing or having a conversation with someone in person, unless I went to maybe the grocery store. That kind of life is not for everyone, but I was comfortable. The Lord created us to be in a relationship with each other. That is exemplified when He said to Adam, *'It is not good that the man should be alone; I will make him an help meet for him.'* ~ Genesis 2:18. Being isolated can make a period of tribulation even more tormenting if we do not have anyone to support us. There are several reasons why solitary confinement is a form of punishment in prison. I remember a song from my early years that basically stated no man is an island and no man stands alone. There are times when the presence of people can result in more troubles and conflicts, but they are also times when others can help us through our tribulations.

I recall a recruitment briefing in the military for a special branch. One of focal points was how members of the branch were capable of functioning as a highly efficient team, but was also capable of functioning individually. That is how I see myself, one who is capable of functioning alone or as a member of a team. In similar way, John 6 outlines how when people departed from Christ, He did not pursue them. The Lord even went further by opening the door for His apostles to leave. He could have found new apostles or simply stood alone. In fact, at the time of His crucifixion, Jesus stood alone. I am willing to stand together with others or alone (with Christ Jesus) if necessary. The enemy tried numerous things to cut me off from others, and he was effective up to a point. Yet, he utterly failed at trying to cut me off from my most important relationship, which is with Christ Jesus. The more I was cut off from people was the closer I drew to the Lord.

Sometimes I marvel at the fact that I have spent so much time alone in the last several years, without being totally socially awkward as a result of that isolation. One such example was when I recently went out of town to attend a family member's retirement ceremony. It served as a mini family reunion of sorts. I spent time with family, and other associates, some of whom I had not seen in at least 20 years. I went from being in a house by myself to a house with 13 other people. Despite the time we had spent apart, and also the time I had spent alone, we meshed very well and kept each other entertained, without any conflicts. There were times when I surprised myself when I made jokes and caused others to laugh. It was good to know I had not lost my sense of humor to the devil. But then again, there were several times during my tribulation that I laughed at the devil for his stupidity. Whatever happens in this life, it is but a vapor compared to eternity. I am bound for heaven while they are destined for inescapable and everlasting torment. I am going to have the last laugh.

When I was away from home, the presence of the enemy was not as strong. Despite enjoying myself, I knew the enemy was watching and my joy was driving him absolutely nuts. My joy, and ability to bring joy to others, after so many awful experiences, was reminiscent of how the preincarnate Christ Jesus protected Shadrach, Meshach, and Abednego when they were cast into the fire. The Lord has protected me and some aspects of my personality have not changed, while purging other things. It certified that despite the enemy's numerous and incessant attempts to destroy me, he had failed. This was a five-day trip and it was wonderful to be around people, without conflict, and for us to share so much joy. It was also very refreshing to eat without having to cook or dine out. I ensured I publicly expressed my gratitude for their efforts. I enjoyed it while it lasted because I knew I was heading back to my former routine, soon. Clearly, the enemy had been attacking my God-given ability to bring joy to others, especially those who are having a hard time seeing the "silver lining in the dark cloud". The devil would love for me to be, or at least appear to be, a miserable minister who drives people away from this ministry to which the Lord has called me, and subsequently away from the Lord.

The trip also gave me a break from ministering to people who are not my blood relatives, and decreased the time I usually spent doing social media ministry. I had a chance to do something I seldom do, which is to minister to members of my family. My feelings about the enemy's misery were proven right on about the third night. After three days of peace, I started hearing the same poltergeist activity in the house I was visiting, but not quite as bold as when I was home to not draw attention to itself. I also knew the enemy was trying to see if any of my family could discern his presence, and their level of spiritual authority. So, on the third night, the enemy started making his presence felt. I started hearing noises in the house and the demonic dreams started coming back, but they were not as frequent or intense. It is what I call "demonic logic" for an entity to be so obsessed with someone it hates, and that person hates it in return. At this point in time, it was still a mystery why this devil had been so attached to me after I had been trying to get rid of it for 10 months. However, one of the things I was able to do during that five-day trip was to get more rest than I had gotten throughout most of the tribulation.

Ironically, the enemy does not want me to have rest or joy because when he is in the lake of fire, he will not find rest, and he certainly will not have joy. The enemy is literally trying to make my life hell on earth. But I find solace knowing that being absent from this body means being present with the Lord, and all these things will have passed away. I will spend eternity in peace and joy while the enemy is suffering. A part of my joy now comes from knowing the enemy will suffer the consequences for everything he has done to me, and, so many other people throughout the ages. Another example of "demonic logic" is devils are trying to take as many people to hell with them, as if the people are going to provide "fire insurance". The more lives these devils destroy is the worse their punishment will be. They have already lost the battle they are fighting, which is a part of why they are in a lose-lose situation. The devil that has been on my case is already in deep trouble in the kingdom of darkness. If it had left me alone 10 months ago, the contents of this book would not be so rich. In addition, if it had left me alone 10 months ago, its punishment from its superiors would not be so great. It is very dangerous to hang around after someone gives you the chance to walk away, and to simply cut your losses and go in peace. If you want a war you risk becoming a casualty.

Misery loves company, but despite having spent so much time with devils all around me, I absolutely refuse to become as miserable as they are. My joy and peace are in and from the Lord. There are some things the enemy can steal, but there are other things he cannot have unless I give it to him. Peace, love, and joy are among the fruit of the Holy Spirit (Galatians 5:22-23). I will eat and enjoy those fruit and I will not share any of it with the devil. Sadly, this type of parasitic relationship with the devil is what some people are experiencing in relationships and even marriages. Some of you can relate because you are in a relationship with someone who is only happy when you are miserable. That person is literally sucking the life out of you because he or she has no life for him or herself. **Misery loves company, but we should not allow others to make us miserable. Divorce the devil.**

Angry Devil

I was working on the manuscript for this book when I had a visitation from a devil. It is fall, but the temperature outside, and consequently in the house, is much colder than expected. However, it is not cold enough for me to turn the heat on yet; I am trying to wait until winter. Well, I was busy getting things done and it suddenly felt hot in the room. Based on the character of a demon, it may manifest as a hateful and heat-filled presence in the room. In some cases, the heat is because the devil is angry with you.

Such a manifestation is a sign that you are doing something right. As a result, a part the devil's response is to try to take authority over you, but you must take authority over him, in the name of Jesus. I keep wondering how much longer before this Scripture proves effective: "Submit yourselves therefore to God. Resist the devil, and he will flee from you." ~ James 4:7. This devil does not want to stay away so I am going to make it pay, dearly. Apparently, this devil is a slow learner, so I am going to spell this out very clearly to him that I have rejected him and his entire kingdom by continuing to resist him every day and in every way.

Another noteworthy thing is that a devil may be attacking, or counterattacking, in an effort to afflict and torment you. A devil's anger is a sign that it is being tormented, which is why it is angry and out for vengeance. Devils want to be like God and therefore seek our worship. Our steadfastness in worshipping the Lord is a source of torment for a devil. It is a sign that it has been wasting its time, and that you have abandoned it in favor of a relationship with Christ Jesus. It is like a former partner leaving to go into a relationship with your worst enemy. Repenting and committing our life to Christ, means the devil has lost his influence and control over us. As a result, there is nothing the devil can do to win us back (John 10:27-30). Do not allow a devil, to steal your peace and joy. Whatever you are doing with and for the Lord, continue doing it for His glory. It is advisable to pray for the Lord's protection, to include for His angels to encamp around you while you are doing His work. Do not allow the devil to get anything from you for free. Whatever he tries taking, or whatever he tries doing, ensure he incurs a cost that is more than he can bear (see Proverbs 6:30-31). In time, the devil will learn to think twice about ever messing with you, or anyone associated with you. The devil will have to count the costs before he plans and executes any operations against you. Develop a reputation of being the person who will strike back as soon as you get the opportunity, just like David. He was a warrior for the Lord, and unlike his predecessor, king Saul, David's enemies knew he would utterly destroy them.

Ministers, Do Not Boast About Conquests

A source of pride among some ministers is speaking of, or even outright bragging, about previous successes. I have heard many ministers speak of casting out devils, major prophecies coming to pass, and of miracles and healings. On the contrary, very few speak about the devil they could not cast out, the prophecy that failed to come to pass (either because the Lord had not spoken, or they misinterpreted what the Lord had communicated), or, the person they prayed for who did not receive a miracle or healing. I respect the one minister who saw the devil I was dealing with and recognized it was out of her league. She then recommended someone she recognized as having more spiritual authority to cast out devils. Regrettably, I did not get free after seeing that minister either. No, these words are not out of bitterness. On the contrary, they are a potent reminder that Christ Jesus is the source of our breakthrough and people are simply His vessels.

When a minister presents his or her successes like a resume, it is worthwhile only if he or she can deliver similar results again. We are not God and our gifts and calling are from the Lord but they are subject to Him instead of us. Consequently, we will always be more successful when we are doing things in accordance with the Lord's will instead of our own. Presenting one's resume of previous conquests is a great motivational tool that gives a person in need of those services great hope. Ministers need humility in part because with the ability to give hope comes the possibility of delivering great disappointment. For example, it is great if we successfully ministered healing and deliverance to others. However, it is not good if we fail to minister healing and/or deliverance to a hopeful candidate with the same affliction. We need to ensure that the Holy Spirit is leading us to whom He wants us to minister to. People are more interested in what we are presently doing now instead of what we did 30 years ago on a crusade in West Africa. It is very disheartening to see a minister, whom professes to have "the goods", but fails to deliver. When a minister fails it looks like Jesus failed, but He never fails, or makes excuses.

A part of why some ministers speak of previous accomplishments is to bolster the faith of others. Sadly, many people have more than enough faith to get healed and/or delivered, but it still does not work. Many people have walked away from the faith because they felt like Jesus failed them. Again, humility and submitting to the Holy Spirit's lordship are important components of a successful ministry. We should exercise caution when speaking of previous successes because if we oversell, we need to deliver. It is better to undersell and over produce, than to oversell and under produce. It is tragic when those who oversell and under produce resort to blaming the person who is seeking ministry as being the issue. For example, the minister may claim the person was not healed or delivered because he or she lacked faith. Despite the fact the person had the faith to come and see the minister to receive the same results the minister purported to have delivered to so many others before. Sometimes the truth is, the minister was operating based on self-will, even attempts at self-aggrandizement, instead of operating under the auspices and unction of the Holy Spirit. As I will discuss in an upcoming segment, healing and deliverance are things people often seek out of sheer desperation. A person with stage four cancer is in a desperate life and death situation. Likewise, a person who has been experiencing demonic manifestations, whether internally and/or externally, and has not slept in a month, is desperate. For the love of God, please, we should not mislead anyone or ourselves by claiming we are the Lord's chosen vessel to heal and/or deliver someone when we are not. We should **ensure that our previous successes do not lead to our future failures because of pride**. Remember, God resists the proud but gives grace to the humble (Proverbs 3:34, James 4:6, etc.).

We ought to model our ministries after Jesus. The Lord did not go around telling people about what He had done while ministering to others. On the contrary, there were times when He ministered to someone and instructed the person not to tell anyone. Maybe some people were simply disobedient, but many people disobeyed the Lord and told others of what He had done. That was a part of how the Lord developed His reputation. He also maintained that reputation by living up to the good things people had said about Him. Likewise, our works should testify of us, and in due time, God will exalt us. We have to be careful that our ministries are more about Christ Jesus than they are about marketing. For instance, have we ministered to people away from the cameras, away from social media, and even without those we are ministering to, knowing our name but instead they know the name of Christ Jesus?

Our gifts will make room for us in front of great men. When we do the work of the Lord, He will put us in positions to minister to others, effectively. In addition, the Lord will manage our reputation and our reputation will precede us. For example, Samuel had a reputation as a prophet whose words surely came to pass (1 Samuel 3:19-20). Daniel was renowned as a wise man, with the Spirit of God, who could unlock the mysteries of dreams and visions (Daniel 4:8-9, 5:11, etc.). They did not have to speak about themselves. The Holy Spirit ensured those they would minister to knew of their reputation as ministers of God. Likewise, Elisha did not tell the Shunnamite woman he was a prophet but she discerned that he was a holy man of God (2 Kings 4). Similarly, Jesus seldom outrightly said He was the Christ; His ways and works helped to testify of that (see John 10:24-32). So, while using our title for example is not out of order, we should examine how we react when people simply call us by our given name. Paul wrote letters by using his name, and then subsequently stated he was an apostle of Christ. He did not start those Epistles by saying "I, the apostle Paul". We also called the Son of God, "Jesus". We call the judge of all heaven and earth simply by His first name, and it is not disrespectful. Yet, it does not take away from the Lord's esteem and sovereignty to call Him by His first name. We need to be careful about trying to build our brand and our reputation. A few people who are now disenfranchised, feeling hopeless, can shatter our years of ministry if we cannot not deliver as advertised.

Whether we realize it or not, speaking of our past successes becomes a promise of being able to deliver in the current situation. Jesus made Himself of no reputation, and so should we. We need to keep Jesus first and foremost, while being mindful of how our words and promises can have a have a negative impact on others, if the Lord does not back us up. People will not generally care about the wonderful works we did for others if we cannot do the same for them in their time of need. I am very leery when I see an advertisement claiming everyone will receive a prophetic word from at a meeting. The Lord may not have something to say to everyone at that time. A prophet who promises to have a word for everyone may either prophesy from his or her soul, or, operate with a familiar spirit that wants to bring attention to the prophet, and subsequently itself. Be forewarned that **any prophet can give you "a word" but Jesus is "The Word"** (John 1:1, 1 John 5:7, etc.). In addition, when it comes to judging a prophecy, it is paramount to remember that '...*the testimony of Jesus is the Spirit of Prophecy.*' ~ Revelation 19:10. A spirit of divination tells people what they want to hear, and it also gives general information that of little value to the person. Sadly, while the spirit may have accurate details about a person's past and present, the things it reveals about a person's future is an attempt to destroy that person's destiny. A prophet operating under the unction of an impure spirit puts everyone he or she ministers to in bondage to the devil. When that prophet puts enough people in bondage to the devil, he will reward the prophet with supernatural power(s). Those are the kind of ministers who usually entice people to come to their event expecting "a major move of God".

We ought to test the spirits because not every spirit is of God (1 John 4:1). Testing the spirits does not always require being in a minister's presence. It is best to test the spirit <u>before</u> venturing into a minister's sphere of influence by asking the Lord about His desires for us. Follow David's example because he would not even go after his captured family without first inquiring of the Lord (1 Samuel 30). While it is said we should not judge a book by its cover, we can tell a lot about someone based on his or her appearance. Sometimes we can see from afar a minister who is oozing with pride or carnality based on his or her appearance, and subsequent conduct. However, do not assume a minister who has good appearance is a carnal minister. For example, "…the love of money is the root of all evil…" ~ 1 Timothy 6:10. But there is a difference between a person having money versus money having the person. Job was wealthy, but when he basically lost it all, his love for the Lord did not change. After Job's tribulation, the Lord even saw it fit to bless him twice as much as before. Interestingly, before the tribulation, here is one of the things the Lord said about His servant Job: *'…there is none like him in the earth, a perfect and an upright man, one that feareth God, and escheweth evil?'* ~ Job 1:8

Demonic Character

Demons are hateful, absolutely full of hate, very jealous and possessive. Arguably, they are most jealous of humans being able to repent while they are condemned. We can commit some of the most egregious sin, repent and earnestly turn to the Lord by asking for His forgiveness, and get washed clean by the blood of Jesus. Unsurprisingly, demons are also very petty. Amazingly, even though the Lord informs us of the devil's devices, he simply repackages the same tricks and keeps presenting them in various ways.

There were times when the Lord allowed me to shut down certain demonic things in dreams and/or visions, but it seemed as if the devil had absolutely nothing better to do than to try to waste my time, and his, by coming back with the same old repackaged tricks. In fact, I had a dream this morning where I was in the back of the U-Haul trailer trying to clear (unload) a 9mm pistol. One of the things about clearing a weapon, especially with my military background, is avoiding an accidental/negligent discharge. It would prompt an investigation if someone fired a round while clearing a weapon. I will not belabor the point, but I conducted several such investigations, even though no one got hurt. Well, in the dream, I had a sense that I needed to carefully clear the weapon without firing a round. While that was my focus, I knew two other people were with me, but I could not see their faces. I remained focused on safely clearing the weapon in the confined space. I also wanted to ensure I did not accidentally fire a round because it could have ricocheted all throughout the trailer and into one of us. The Lord has given me lots of training regarding how the enemy thinks. Therefore, I discerned after waking up that the enemy wanted me to focus on clearing the weapon; in a situation he rigged. I also realized I had not done one of the first steps in clearing a pistol. I had not removed the magazine from its well to prevent another round from replacing the ejected one in the chamber. This was another classic setup from the enemy so everything that could go wrong would go wrong. The devil wanted me to focus on something minor, so I would not discern what his main effort of attack was. The enemy was trying to disarm me as I was becoming more powerful in the spirit (as we would say). In fact, he was trying to get me to work against myself by disarming myself. The enemy was threatened because, like Samson, I was regaining my strength (Judges 16). I was in fact breaking free of the enemy's sorcery that he had been using to gain dominance over me while I slept. The enemy was also trying to convince me that I lacked competence to handle any power and authority the Lord wanted to bestow upon me. It is important to note that the Lord does not allow His children to come out of a trial without rewarding them handsomely.

A benefit to the magazine remaining in the weapon meant I had not been disarmed. The enemy is not the only one who is capable of projecting fiery darts. According to Ephesians 6, we tend to think of fiery darts as being flaming arrows. However, when applied to modern-day combat, a fiery dart also applies to the hot projectile that comes out of a weapon system. Moreover, the enemy was employing several covert schemes and maneuvers. When we carefully look at this scenario, I was in the back of a

U-Haul trailer and the door was (presumably) closed. That represents being caged or imprisoned by the enemy. This would prevent me from doing the things the Lord had called me to do. In addition, the U-Haul trailer meant the enemy had the ability to take me wherever he pleased. Therefore, the devil wanted to usurp the Jesus' authority by taking over the lordship of my life. Since I was more focused on clearing the weapon instead of escaping, the devil wanted to claim I had given him authority over me. [*The devil is devious and will try to steal what we will not freely give to him.*] The enemy was trying to take me where he pleased. It meant he would prevent me from connecting with people the Lord has ordained for me to minster to, or, receive ministry from. The devil was also trying to keep me in the dark regarding the things the Lord has for me. While the inside looked like a trailer, the outside could have been a coffin. I have had several dreams where the enemy was trying to get me to form a covenant with death, so he could kill me, and subsequently this ministry.

I say the enemy is petty is because I have knowledge about his plans and operations but he keeps trying to trick me. But, thanks to the Lord's help, I am exposing the devil's treachery. I have publicly stated that I refuse to forge or maintain any covenants with the devil. As a result, if I do not reject and destroy those covenants before the enemy tries forging them with me in an encounter, I will rebuke and reject them as soon as I come to my senses. It is like the prodigal son who is working in a man's pigsty. However, he came to his senses, renounced his covenant with the farmer, and returned to his father's house. I keep running back to my Heavenly Father's house while the enemy is trying to get me to do things I have no desire for. This was after the Lord told me to not return to my vomit. I am also clearly instructed to "…have no fellowship with the unfruitful works of darkness, but rather reprove them." ~ Ephesians 5:11. Subsequently, as soon as I came to my senses, I basically said, "satan, the Lord Jesus Christ rebuke you, the Lord Jesus Christ rebuke you, the Lord Jesus Christ rebuke you."

As a precaution, I frequently renounce demonic covenants even if I am not sure I had a demonic encounter. This spiritual warfare is too intense for me to "under pray". Again, **Prayer is a weapon.** I try my best to flee and avoid all forms of sin, but the enemy keeps bringing sin to me. The enemy is like water that is trying to break down rock, regardless of how long it takes. Therefore, I stay out of the water or get the water away from me. It is reminiscent of how Potiphar's wife kept trying to seduce Joseph after he (continually) rejected her. Joseph did not want to dishonor his earthly master or sin against the Lord his God, but she kept pestering him. Even when Joseph did the right thing by running away from her, she would not stop. She was a messenger of satan who tried to destroy Joseph, especially because she could not have him. The vixen played the victim by claiming Joseph tried to sexually assault her. The Lord allowed Joseph to serve the rest of his "developmental time" in prison. Potiphar's wife thought she had destroyed Joseph but she actually helped to propel him towards his God-ordained destiny. The story demonstrates how the enemy can try his best to derail our destiny, but the Lord knows where we are and what He needs to do to get us where He wants us to be. Rest assured, **the devil's plans will ultimately fail (Isaiah 14:12-27, Luke 10:19, Revelation 20:10, etc.). God is Sovereign and His plans always prevail (Proverbs 19:21). No one can thwart the Lord plans (Job 42:2), no one can annul the Lord's plans (Isaiah 14:27), and His Words will accomplish His intended purpose (Isaiah 55:8-11).** The Lord will fulfill His promises, despite the enemy's best efforts. Also, lest not forget that after years of suffering, when the Lord redeemed Joseph, he was the second to the pharaoh, which meant his former boss Potiphar, and his wicked wife, were below Joseph. God is a righteous God, and He loves justice.

The Lord prepared a table for David in the presence of his enemies (Psalm 23:5). So do not consider it strange if the Lord allows your enemies to stay around to witness Him blessing you, abundantly. It also demonstrates His goodness and power to your (former) human persecutors. The Lord allowed the Egyptians to see how He parted the Red Sea so His Israelite children could walk across safely on dry ground. However, similarly to how the Lord used the same pathway to crush the Egyptians, He may use your blessings to utterly destroy the enemy. Sometimes the Lord allows you to see how He handles your (former) enemies, which were His enemies too. Praise the Lord for when He delivers, but do not gloat over your fallen enemy:

> "For a just man falleth seven times, and riseth up again: but the wicked shall fall into mischief. Rejoice not when thine enemy falleth, and let not thine heart be glad when he stumbleth: Lest

the Lord see it, and it displease Him, and He turn away His wrath from him. Fret not thyself because of evil men, neither be thou envious at the wicked: For there shall be no reward to the evil man; the candle of the wicked shall be put out." ~ Proverbs 24:16-20

I use these words to describe devils: Sneaky. Stubborn. Spiteful. Shameless.

Delayed Deliverance

As previously discussed, every worker of iniquity is in serious bondage to the devil. Even though deserving of damnation, as were we, they also deserve fervent prayer that they would repent and accept Christ Jesus as their Lord and Savior. One of the reasons why deliverance may take longer is because even though we are suffering, we are actually keeping our enemy alive. For example, Jesus spoke about giving Jezebel time to repent (Revelation 2:18-23). She failed to repent by the appointed time so He imposed the death penalty upon her, her cohorts, and her children. However, it is not always the Lord who directly executes judgment on workers of iniquity. As a result of their bondage to the devil, he may kill them if they fail an assignment. Their attacks are oftentimes so relentless because their life depends on a favorable outcome. It will not be pleasant, but since the Lord knows we are saved and will be in heaven with Him, He graciously gives the worker of iniquity as much time as possible to repent and come to Him. We may not realize that the way we conduct ourselves, including showing love to our enemy, could potentially win that enemy over because of the graciousness of our actions. Unfortunately, for a hardened enemy, that person may view our gracious actions as a sign of weakness. But the Lord has a plan for that too, which plays a role in that person's judgment.

The Kingdom of God is referred to as an upside down kingdom. That is not to say it is in disarray. On the contrary, it is a kingdom of order, pristine order. It is an upside down kingdom in part because the Lord exalts the humble and He expects leaders to serve instead of being served. In the devil's kingdom, entities basically have to gather souls and make others subject to them in order to secure their advancement. Sadly, if they fail to make their quotas, they will suffer serious consequences, which may include death. Therefore the Lord may delay our deliverance in an effort to save the human emissary of the enemy who has been fighting against us. Despite the person's vigorous attempts to ruin our life, he or she is benefiting from us being like a life support machine that is keeping him or her alive. An example of this is David and Saul. Saul tried to kill David on multiple occasions over the years. David could not find peace in Israel as long as Saul was alive. Therefore, David took the drastic measure of going to live with the Philistines, in Gath, for 16 months where he found peace from Saul's persecution (1 Samuel 27). Imagine that, two men who believed in the true and living God, but one of them had to go and live with the enemy in order to find peace. Just in case you missed it, I mentioned Gath because that was Goliath's hometown (1 Samuel 17:4).

I can relate to David because much of my warfare occurred in my own bedroom. In addition, I had more peace when I was away from the home the Lord had blessed me with. Unlike David, we cannot go to the enemy's camp to find peace. In addition, in order for us to find peace, the Lord may have to permanently remove our enemies. In many ways, spiritual warfare is a life and death struggle. One of the best outcomes is for the person who is serving the devil, by working against us, to repent. But sometimes the person has to die so we can move on to the things the Lord has called us to do. Such was the case with David, who would have never become king as long as Saul was alive. A part of why king Saul died was that he fell upon his own sword. Likewise, unrepentant workers of iniquity will fall upon their own sword, or the devil's.

Jesus died to potentially save every person, but His ultimate responsibility is to save His children from the evils of this world. The Lord said He would return to separate the sheep from the goats, and He would send the goats to hell along with the devils they served. A time will come when we will all face judgment for our actions, chief among those actions is whether we accepted Christ as our Lord and Savior and kept His commandments. Do not make the mistake of taking Jesus lightly, to include taking His grace for granted. When the Lord said vengeance was His and He would recompense, He meant it. He is a God of righteousness, justice, and judgment. In order for us to advance, our enemies may have to perish; the choice is theirs.

For any worker of iniquity who reads this, it does not matter what kind a covenant you have made with the devil, or what you have done while serving him, Jesus can set you free from bondage. The Lord Jesus Christ can break every covenant you have made with the devil. I know devils have a way of claiming ownership because of covenants. However, there is room at the cross for you. Once your name is written in the Lamb's Book of Life, there is no place in the devil's book of death for you. Jesus sacrificed Himself to save and redeem all of you. When He redeems you, He permanently translates you from the kingdom of darkness into His kingdom of light. Once you bear the marks of Christ, it will not matter what you have done for the devil in the past. You become a new creation, one who belongs to Jesus, wholeheartedly. It does not matter if you have a tattoo or a carving of a pentagram on our chest, you belong to Christ Jesus, completely, and our covenants with the devil are broken.

Deuteronomy 24:1-4 has the Mosaic Law regarding divorce and remarriage. It mentions that if a man found something unclean in his new bride, he could give her a writ of divorcement, and put her out of his tent and life. The writ of divorcement cleared her to legally marry another man. Once she married another man, if that marriage ended by death or divorce, she could not go back to her first husband after being defiled by another man. Similarly, once you divorce the devil, and become a part of the bride of Christ, you belong to Jesus. Therefore, your former husband, the devil, has no more claims to you. I urge you to divorce the devil and seek a relationship with Christ Jesus instead. Jesus is the only one who gave His life up for you. So, if the devil comes knocking, trying to reclaim you as his "bride", he will not be able to get you away from the Lord your God. Again, the devil does not have more authority than Christ Jesus, and when you become the Lord's, you are His. Thus, all previous demonic covenants are broken and you become exclusively, Christ Jesus' and His alone. When Saul gave Michal to Phaltiel, David could reclaim her because he had paid the price for her, two times over, plus since he had not divorced her, she was still his wife. In addition, David was the king, the supreme ruler of the land. Likewise, Jesus the Christ is the only one who has paid the price for you, many times over, and He will not leave or forsake you. Despite your many sins, He can continually redeem you. Jesus is the Redeemer, and King of kings. However, out of respect for His sacrifices, His shed blood, we do not abuse His grace but we certainly give Him thanks and praises for it.

CHAPTER 5

DELIVERANCE CONFERENCE

'For false Christs and false prophets shall rise, and shall shew signs and wonders, to seduce, if it were possible, even the elect.' ~ Jesus (Mark 13:22)

Several people faithfully believed simply touching the hem of Jesus' garments would heal their afflictions. Chief among them was the woman with the issue of blood. She famously touched Jesus' garments and was immediately healed of her 12-yearlong affliction. Touching the hem of Jesus' garment is indicative of being on one's hands and knees, which is an act of desperation to crawl to the source of hope for healing, salvation, and/or deliverance. I was that desperate for the Lord to deliver me.

In the summer of 2018, I received a commentary about a minister who is a gift from God, a modern deliverer, like Moses was to the Israelites. I wondered if the Lord that He had selected the minister to deliver me. I looked up the minister on YouTube and saw some of the deliverance she had ministered. I questioned some of her methods, but the results seemed effective. However, effective deliverance is measured by long-term results. Experientially, I knew what it was like to receive deliverance that only lasted a few hours or days. Despite the questionable practices, it seemed as if the minister had the goods to deliver, not only to get people free, but also to keep them free. Sometimes Jesus delivered people from demonic oppression, or outright possession, and He commanded the demons to leave the people and never return. Mind you, I had ministers who commanded the devils to leave me in the name of Jesus, but they still returned. One such example is a minister who delivered me from a spirit of witchcraft in 2016. I saw the same minister in 2017 and he delivered me from the same spirit of witchcraft, courtesy of the same witch. Anyone who has experienced that, especially after seemingly closing the door the enemy used to gain entrance, may feel very discouraged. Actually, a part of the enemy's strategy, is to make people feel hopeless and give up. Have you ever come across a person who is seemingly full of hopes and dreams, yet lack the drive to even attempt to put those things into action? **Failure has a way of handcuffing a person to the past and making him or her reluctant to reach for the future, even after being set free.**

I was willing to fly to the Bahamas to see if the minister was God's chosen vessel to deliver me. I wanted an immediate end to my torment. I watched some of her videos on YouTube and actually received a measure of deliverance. One of the things I liked about this professing prophetess was how she imposed judgment on the witches who had put people in bondage. I never received any verifiable information about any of those witches either repenting or being punished, but I thought it was an interesting aspect of her ministry. Her administering judgment in the name of the Lord was reminiscent of Jeremiah 28. That was when the Lord had the prophet Jeremiah impose judgment on the (false) prophet Hananiah. For me, it also gave me an ulterior motive to get delivered. It seemed like it would provide an international stage to show that the apostle/prophetess who had been coming against me was not only false, she was a witch. I did not think those thoughts because I was seeking revenge, or at least I do not think so, but I saw it as a potential stage for the Lord to impose His judgment on the witch. My primary focus was on getting delivered. I also realized the deliverance minister would make a spectacle of me during the deliverance process. I simply saw it as another mechanism for the Lord to kill any pride that was in me, which potentially threatened our relationship. I was willing for the Lord to humble me, even more than before. Believe me, my experiences battling the witch have been very humbling.

I liked the way the minister seemingly tormented the devils during the deliverance process, even though sometimes it went on for too long. For me, the torment should give the devils an incentive to never even consider returning to me. I still want every devil that afflicted me to suffer almost as much as the satan. So again, I was willing to fly all the way to the Bahamas to see the prophetess for my deliverance. However, all of my plans to fly to the Bahamas failed miserably. It seemed like a blessing that the minister was coming to the United States for a 3-day deliverance conference. I had enough airline miles to book a round-trip ticket, for free, to go to the deliverance conference. I simply needed to pay for the hotel accommodations and a vehicle for transportation. It seemed like a gift from God, perfectly coordinated for my deliverance. Yet, I was cautiously optimistic for several reasons. Among those reasons was I had seen six other ministers for deliverance. Interestingly, the prophetess said many ministers can call out (identify) a devil but they cannot cast it out, which was something I had experienced. But even worse, ministers had cast devils out of me but could not keep them out. I realize I may have been a special case. As previously stated, my hedge of protection from God was down, so like Job, the devils were free to operate within the confines the Lord had established for them during this season. Despite previous failures, I had renewed hope. It seemed as if the minister could cast out the devils, and torment them in the process so they would not dare return. It is worthy to note how the prophetess from the Bahamas resembled the witch who had been stalking me here in the United States. They were both short stocky women with matching complexion, and even similarly shaped heads. Could it be the Lord was going to use the witch's doppelganger to deliver me?

A witch who is working against you will deploy or employ at least one demon to monitor you and report your activities to the witch. Wielding that power gives a witch a false sense of having authority over the devils. The truth is, the devils are in control. They are simply empowering the witch to secure the witch's damnation, and to gain rights to the witch's offspring down to the third or fourth generation (Exodus 20:3-5). Many witches do not realize that regardless of how much a demon does for them, the demon is serving themselves, and ultimately, satan. To a devil, a witch is like the skin on a snake. Once the snake outgrows the skin, it sheds and discards the skin. Likewise, when the demon has used the witch to his or her full potential, or the length of their contract, the devil kills the hell-bound witch, and moves on. Appeasing the devil with blood sacrifices may extend the witch's life, but the charade always comes to a very tragic end.

Many deceived souls have discovered the devil's promise of reigning in hell with him was grossly overstated. Tragically, some people are struggling because a family member engaged in witchcraft and sold that person's soul to the devil, sometimes three to four generations ago. The only person who benefits from a demonic covenant is the devil. Everything the devil gives is like a hook on a line. A person who takes the bait will not be able to keep anything the devil gives because he is going to call everything back to himself. Subsequently, he will simply discard the person when he is finished and move on to someone else, in some cases, a family member. Jesus came that we may have life more abundantly. On the contrary, the devil came to steal, kill, and destroy. There are no long-term benefits to serving the devil. A person can only take you where he or she is going, and according to Revelation 20:10, the devil will be cast into the lake of fire and be tormented forever and ever. There truly is no benefit to working for a "king" who will not even be the king of his own "kingdom". The devil will suffer everlasting torment.

I was filled with renewed hope of getting delivered. There were a few complications along the way, but it seemed as if the Lord (miraculously) opened some doors for me. I was within a week of leaving when I came across a trailer about the rise of Jezebel, which featured the prophetess I was about to see. Was it a warning from the Lord or bad publicity? Based on what I experienced in 2015, I was willing to cut my losses if the Lord did not want me to go. Unlike in 2015 when the Lord told me to get in my car and leave, I did not get such a clear warning from the Lord about this venture. However, I covered myself in prayer to not come into agreement with anything that was not of the Lord in the conference. The Lord has inspired me to write many things, some of which are scheduled up to six months in advance on either or both of my professional Facebook pages. One of those writings contradicted something about the prophetess' ministry. I rescheduled that post for the day I left for the conference. I was going to find out if I had heard from the Lord on that post or learn if He had given the prophetess some special ability (authority).

Witches monitor people, which is a part of why they know when a spiritual link between them and others get broken. Consequently, I was not shocked when I checked into the hotel and the witch, still posing as a minister of Christ, had a commented on one of my blog posts. I am not sure what she wrote because I had stopped receiving anything from her years ago. I also realized she was using written communications to project witchcraft towards me. She had elevated her game from simply trying to deliver false prophecies, to include lies that the Lord was going to bring judgment upon me for not marrying her. It had gotten to the point where evil spirits were attached to her messages. That was a part of why she kept creating fake social media accounts after I blocked her at least 10 times on Facebook... I already discussed this topic at length in the third chapter of "So, You Want to be a Prophet... ARE YOU CRAZY?"

The days were long at the conference. Yet, delightfully, one of positive things was I slept better than I had in months, even though I did not have a lot of time to sleep. I even had a dream from the Lord reaffirming that this was my year of victory. I was desperate for deliverance, but I did not leave my discernment at home, or even in the hotel room, during the conference. I literally noticed several red flags as soon as I entered the conference area. I know conferences, especially on this scale, require funding to produce and execute, but I still found the merchandizing alarming. Going in and out of the conference rooms basically required walking through the Red Sea (of merchandise and advertisements). What really got me was one day I was walking through the area and the Lord reminded me of what He said in Matthew 7:21-23. I knew that despite the apparent success of the ministry, the prophetess and her husband, an apostle, were in trouble with the Lord. I later realized a part of why the Lord allowed me to go to the conference was to show me what the witch wanted to do. She wanted us to get married so I could be her covering while she acted like the submissive wife. I would be the figurehead and sideshow, while she could be the main attraction. My refusal to cooperate had seriously wrecked her plans for a demonic ministry with demonic children.

Even before I attended the conference, I saw the need for powerful deliverance ministers and ministries here in United States. What the Lord said in Hosea 4:6 applies to many churches in America. Many churches in less developed nations are well aware of the enemy's activities, and therefore better equipped to counteract them. I was at a Christian fellowship early in 2018 when I spoke of being subjected to witchcraft attacks. A lady in the small group left because she did not even want to hear about it, as if ignoring the devil means he will go away. Prior to the conference, many people commented on the minister's videos regarding how excited they were because they could not find deliverance in their local areas. In some cases, that is an indictment against the ministers who do not believe in the gifts of the Holy Spirit. Many people who are gifted to do deliverance have been put out while others were banned from churches. Those institutions traded the power of God for feel-good messages and programs. It is reminiscent of Esau selling his birthright for some lentil stew to satisfy momentary hunger. A part of the state of the (American) church is devils feel at home instead of being uncomfortable. During the deliverance conference, a lady had some wicked spirits. After the deliverance session, when the lady had come to herself, she testified of having traveled to several states, seeking deliverance but not finding it. The lady was allegedly called as an evangelist, but rather than setting people free, she was in bondage to the devil. I wonder how many emergent ministers are in bondage to the devil, and is this the reason why their ministries cannot get started or grow? The deliverance session provided an incredible stage for the minister to show her anointing with respect to ministering deliverance.

I was very excited on the second day when the prophetess asked those who have been battling "spirit spouses" to stand up. I was not ashamed to stand up because I needed help. In fact, being delivered from a spirit that was trying to be my spouse was the primary reason why I was there. I did everything I was told to do to get rid of a "spirit spouse", things that worked for others, but they did not work for me. The minister said she was going to do a deliverance session for spirit spouses the next morning. However, she did not conduct that session as promised. I could not complain because one of the (seemingly) positive things I noticed was she ministered for about 12 continuous hours on the third day. Unlike me, she did not even take a bathroom break. The marathon ministerial session made it appear as if she had a passion to set people free. However, a part of testing the spirits is to determine a person's motive(s). A deliverance minister will encounter many people who are desperate for deliverance, and I most certainly was among them. For an unscrupulous minister, it presents tremendous opportunities to take advantage of people who are desperate for help. Sadly, some deliverance ministries are putting people in bondage to the devil instead of liberating them from him. Consequently, it is important to let the Lord lead us to whoever He will have deliver us.

Overall, we should never forget that ultimately, the Lord is the Deliverer.

Sometimes Jesus wants all the glory for our deliverance. For instance, I give Jesus all the credit for delivering me from the spirit of masturbation. He did not use a minister as an intermediary, which is a part of why the deliverance was so effective. There are times however when He uses ministers with that level of effectiveness. I am inspired to say this to those who have and will have encounters with legitimate ministers of Christ with a strong anointing to do deliverance. Deliverance ministers face a tremendous amount of spiritual warfare, and this includes rejection in many churches. In addition, if they have a church, the congregation is usually transitional, which means people go there to get delivered and then move on. Consequently, I urge you to support legitimate deliverance ministries, primarily with prayer for the Lord's strength and protection. Secondarily, do not to follow the example of the 9 of the 10 lepers Jesus healed who did not return to thank Him (Luke 17:11-19). We should provide as much financial support as we can to these ministers. Very often, a demonic oppression extends to a person's financial resources. However, when a person is delivered, and those resources are restored, they forget about the deliverance minister. In some cases, people are paying tithes to a church where they remained in bondage, but will not give anything to the minister the Lord used to set them free. My outspokenness is a part of why I have so much spiritual warfare, but here I go again on another very controversial topic. Please study Deuteronomy 14:22-29 to see the true correlation between tithes and money. So many ministers will preach about tithing based on Malachi 3:8-12 without sharing the supporting facts, and especially the contradictory facts about tithing. That is a part of what the Lord meant when He said He called me to set the captives free. He inspired me to write a book several years ago called "Knowledge is Power", which epitomizes the following Scripture: "An hypocrite with his mouth destroyeth his neighbour: but **through knowledge shall the just be delivered**." ~ Proverbs 11:9.

It is good to give credit where credit is due, and this includes saying the Lord used a particular minister to help deliver us. We must however ensure we do not give God's glory to another, which is how some ministers go astray because they become proud. Pride is a sneaky devil that has led many ministers to either erecting themselves as idols or allowing others to idolize them. It also masquerades as a form of humility that is actually false humility. I also noticed excessive praise was going to the ministers of that ministry. Traditionally, the apostle ministered first and his wife made an entrance a bit later. However, even though he was in the room ministering, everyone stood up when she entered the room.

During the conference, I usually sat in the very back of the room, even though I showed up earlier than most people. One day, I was sitting in my usual spot when someone from the ministry team did what many ushers had unsuccessfully tried on several occasions, she offered to seat me closer towards the front of the room. When you look at my photograph on "Raised in the Wilderness: Rogue Reformers, Rallying the Remnant", my face is covered by a hood. One of the reasons was because I was in "the wilderness", or having in "the cave experience" as some would say. So when the minister invited me forward, I declined as in times past because my hour had not yet come. However, something was different that time. The Lord spoke through the minister to let me know it was time for me to come out of the cave. It was time for me to stop hanging out in the back because He had called me to the front, to lead. Moving to the front of the conference room served as a prophetic action of me coming out of obscurity and moving forward with my Godly calling.

Deliverance training was on the last day of the conference. Even though I had moved forward the day before, I did not have a chance to return to the back like the previous day. We lined up upside and filed in, which was how I ended up sitting the closest to the front than I had ever been. I was still seeking deliverance even though several things were not to my liking. We were in praise and worship, "setting the atmosphere", which may have contributed to me sleeping so well while I was there. In addition, I may have prayed more than I had ever prayed in a three-day period in my life, at least up until that point of my life. But I was still a rebel so to speak. We had sat down prior to the prophetess entering the room. Then came the announcement for everyone to stand for the prophetess, but I remained seated. The next thing I knew, an eagle-eyed usher came and politely asked me to please stand for the prophetess. If I did not need deliverance, and thought she was capable of doing it, I would have remained seated, which probably would have gotten me thrown out. But, because I was desperate and still needed deliverance, I got up. I also complied because I stood up when a senior commander entered the room when I was in the military. I addition, I spoke to the Lord, just in case I was in error, based on when Naaman said to Elisha after being healed of leprosy, which was also a factor in something that happened towards the end of the day:

> '...Thy servant will henceforth offer neither burnt offering nor sacrifice unto other gods, but unto the Lord. In this thing the Lord pardon thy servant, that when my master goeth into the house of Rimmon to worship there, and he leaneth on my hand, and I bow myself in the house of Rimmon: when I bow down myself in the house of Rimmon, the Lord pardon thy servant in this thing.' ~ 2 Kings 5:17-18

I can only do some things for a limited time before I become saturated and can no longer go along with "the program". Many people in churches are saturated with some of the chicanery. But they feel powerless to do anything, to include leave, so they remain in bondage, silently suffering inside.

Going to the conference marked me coming out of the cave in many ways, even though I remained at its mouth for a while. The conference also marked the last time I would ever tolerate certain things. The Lord spoke to me directly about His plans for me during the conference, which is why no one should chase after prophets for prophecies. I was on edge when He said I needed to say what He tells me to say, and when. I knew it meant He was going to use me to say things at times I will be uncomfortable with. Nonetheless, I have to deliver the Word of the Lord, upon His command. In fact, I was going to remove the references to the deliverance minister being from the Bahamas. Then the Lord gently reminded me of what He had said. I also remember the poem I was inspired to write about the late Dr. Maya Angelou in "Knowledge is Power". I was inspired to write the poem a year prior to her passing when the Lord told me He was getting ready to call her home. To make a long story short, the original title was "Rest In Peace Dr. Angelou", but I changed it "Rest Dr. Angelou" shortly before the book was published 12 months later. Dr. Angelou passed away about a month after "Knowledge is Power" was published.

About two months after the conference, the Lord used me to deliver one of those messages. I was praying while driving to a business meeting when the Lord instructed me to speak out against professing Christians who practice yoga. I knew the message was not going to be taken well, especially based on how the Lord told me to deliver it. When the leader of the meeting wanted someone to pray at its commencement, I did. It was also the way the Lord had instructed me to deliver the message. A part of that prayer was saying most people do not have the guts to outright tell Jesus that they hate Him. Yet, they show Him with their actions, such as practicing yoga. One can practice Hinduism without practicing yoga, but a person cannot practice yoga without practicing Hinduism. Therefore, yoga is ultimately idolatry. For example, when a person does a salutation, that individual is saluting another god, who is no god at all, but is a devil seeking worship.

That ties into a major event during the closing moments of the conference, something many people did not even realize. We got on the ground, on both knees including the prophetess. It was like we were around a campfire, relaxing, but then the prophetess got up and everyone was told to remain on the floor, on their knees. Outwardly, it seemed innocuous, but the dynamic changed to where it seemed as if we were bowing down to the prophetess. Many people mistake worship for raising their hands to the Lord. However, Biblically, worship means to bow down, for example:

"And **I** [John] **fell at his feet to worship him**.

And he [an angel] said unto me, *'See thou do it not: I am thy fellowservant, and of thy brethren that have the testimony of Jesus: worship God: for the testimony of Jesus is the spirit of prophecy.'"* ~ Revelation 19:10

The angel of the Lord did not want John to worship him. We had been subtly placed in a position of worship when the prophetess stood up while we remained on our knees. I did not get all of this at the time, but I felt uncomfortable with being on both my knees, so I stood up and knelt on one knee. In the military, taking one knee is also a position used to fire a weapon. My modified stance was one of defiance. I received even greater clarity after the conference; the Holy Spirit is an excellent teacher. Other red flags littered the field of play so to speak. Some people would describe the events on that day as being "a powerful move of God", but something got my attention and it was a good thing it happened on the last day. In fact, during the entire conference, I kept asking the Lord if I should leave based on some observations. I had other productive things I could have done in that region outside of the conference. Yet, staying until the end placed me in a great position to observe a lot.

I felt a measure of deliverance in many areas including when the minister identified a "spirit of torment" that had been afflicting me, hence the sleep deprivation. Conversely, I was alarmed when the minister began twirling and said no one should touch her, then she began waving around a piece of cloth like what Benny Him does with his jacket. I saw people falling back and I wondered if they were faking it, like when her husband pushed people backwards like he was taking a free throw while playing basketball. I often saw people falling down out of ritualism instead of a minister's spiritual power. To my surprise, the minister stood at a distance and moved her hand towards me, as if throwing something into the area where the demonic manifestation had been going on in my lower left quadrant of my abdomen. I felt a powerful force hit my body, about two to three times, driving me back and almost knocked me to the ground. I am a strong man who has squatted more than 600 pounds and leg pressed almost 2000 pounds in my life. Yet, it took just about all of my strength to keep on my feet. Based on that experience, I can say some ministers do wield a force that knocks people down, but it is not the Holy Spirit or one of the Lord's angels.

I prayed to cover myself from any ungodly forces during the conference, which may explain why I was not knocked down. I also told the Lord I refuse to come into agreement with any false prophecies or prophets. While the Lord may honor such prayers, it is best to avoid going into questionable environments. We should stay away from places where the Lord's grace will not cover us. In some cases, the Lord will allow us to suffer the consequences of certain actions so that we will not do things outside of His will and direction. In this case, the Lord allowed me to have this experience so that I would know the truth. Attending the conference confirmed a lesson I had learned about exercising caution when exposing ministers. Some receive demonic assistance that we may not be prepared to handle. Have you ever wondered why Elijah demonstrated God's awesome power while defeating the 450 false prophets on Mount Carmel (1 Kings 18), yet, that same "powerful man of God" (as we like to say nowadays), ran from Jezebel after she threatened his life? The prophet even asked the Lord to kill him (1 Kings 19:1-4). However, Elijah came out of the cave, "mouth first", and pronounced the Lord's judgment against the evil queen Jezebel. The newly crowned Jehu later imposed that judgment. The Lord used a king to depose an evil queen.

It serves as an example that we may see error but it may not be the Lord's will or timing for us to expose it. He may have us pronounce judgment but have someone else execute it. In fact, Jehu gave the order to throw down Jezebel, which her eunuchs executed. A part of why the Lord does things this way is based on the enemy's backlash, which some people are not equipped to handle. Some ministers are liars while others are working with demonic powers, some more powerful than others. Even though the Lord invests time and effort into developing His ministers, and also protects them, the devil does the same thing with his ministers. A few months after the conference, Sam Medina said he was working on a book called "Exposing the False Prophet: A Field Guide for Defending the Flock". If he had published that book prior to the conference, I would not have attended.

I have been through many things that I have hated. However, those experiences equipped me in ways I would not trade for the world. For example, I can write this book from a position of having experienced these things. Moses is credited with writing the first five Books of the Bible, which include the Book of Genesis. Moses wrote about the creation of the world, even though he was not physically present at the time. Likewise, John wrote of the end of the world, even though it had not happened. So, the Lord could have revealed these things to me in a dream or a vision. He could have also simply given me these notes, or at least most of them, to tell a story of the things the devil has done and is doing to His children, but there is a certain character to a story when it is based on personal experiences. The Lord also knows I will say things others will not, even if I end up looking bad in the process. "The Anatomy of a Heartbreak: When SAMson met Delilah" was the first book I was ever inspired to write. It has things that do not make me look good. Likewise, this book is a compilation of hundreds of pages from my journal entries, things I personally experienced. Some people have had worse experiences, and my ordeal allows me to empathize. The Lord allowed me to experience things in part because He knew I would not be afraid or shamed to write and speak about them. Another thing I can empathize with was when Jesus said to Peter,

'Simon, Simon, behold, satan hath desired to have you, that he may sift you as wheat: But I have prayed for thee, that thy faith fail not: and when thou art converted, strengthen thy brethren.' ~ Luke 22:31-32

I left the conference feeling great, but mostly because of the things the Lord had revealed to me about His plans for me. In addition, the Lord fulfilled a part of a dream He had given me about 15 months prior, which was one of the most special things that happened while I was in that region. The spirit and the witch that were trying to be my spouse would remain a thorn in my flesh for a little longer, but I knew their days were numbered. The Lord knew how and when He would deliver me, I simply had to rely on His way and timing. He had also shown me how the witch would meet her end, also in due time.

I had a dream on the return flight that radically disrupted my peace. I dreamt I was back on the highway, driving to the airport, just like I had driven a few hours prior. There were no other cars on the highway in front of mine. I could drive as fast as I wanted, in any lane I desired. But I drove around a corner and saw the "prophetess" standing in the middle of the highway, as if to resist me. The devil did not want me to have the freedom of maneuver to advance towards my destiny, but I am too familiar with Revelation 3:7-8:

> "And to the angel of the church in Philadelphia write; These things saith He [Jesus] that is holy, He that is true, He that hath the key of David, He that openeth, and no man shutteth; and shutteth, and no man openeth; *'I know thy works: behold,* **I have set before thee an open door, and no man can shut it:** *for thou hast a little strength, and hast kept My Word, and hast not denied My name.'"*

Oftentimes, when the Lord opens a door for us, the devil tries to block it or us from seeing it, and even walking through it. When the Lord told the Israelites to go and possess the Promised Land, most were too afraid of the sons of Anak, the giants in the land, hence the 40-year delay in reaping the promise (Numbers 13-14).

The dream was reflective of how people seek deliverance but sometimes end up in a worse condition. If the deliverance minister is a messenger of satan, the minister may set someone free, temporarily. Sometimes by casting out most of the devils but leaving one as a gatekeeper. Consequently, even if a person goes and sin no more, the individual will have a devil keeping an open door for other devils to exploit. The minister may also put the devils in a dormant state, thereby making the person believe he or she was delivered, but the devils are simply lying low, leaving the person asymptomatic. That is why we may hear of some people being healed of cancer but end up dying of the same type of cancer a few months later, as if the disease (spirit) came back with a vengeance. In other cases, the minister either replaces the old devils with new and wickeder devils, or, adds those devils to the existing ones. Sadly, under the authority of an evil "deliverance minister", the person ends up in a worse condition. **Some "deliverance ministers" only deliver people to satan.** These are some of the ways that the devil works. When people either knowingly or unknowingly seeks him, or one of his emissaries, they will always get more than they bargained for. Every demonic contract or covenant comes with fine print that puts a person in bondage to the devil, even if they did not know they had sought the devil for help.

While it may seem as if what I saw in the dream was only a dream, I have had too many supernatural experiences to discount any of them, whether they are from God, my soul, or the devil. In the case of the latter, I am now more familiar with what to do with these encounters. I also know the Lord will confirm things in the natural realm. I felt as if I should go through deliverance after attending the deliverance conference, just in case the Lord did not answer my prayers for protection beforehand. The Lord had answered my prayers, but not according to my desire, and for very good reasons. So I called into the deliverance line of the previous ministry that had worked with me. I got through and one of the things the minister mentioned, without knowing I had been to the conference, was about spiritually disconnecting me from the false prophetess. It confirmed I had been playing in the devil's playground. In addition, another minister from the Bahamas did a video on the antics of the minister I had seen. It served as confirmation, even though I did not need it

I learned many hard lessons the hard way. As a result, I stopped seeking deliverance, including from the ministry that had been very helpful for much of the year. Instead, I turned to the Lord, and Him alone, and asked Him to deliver me. I did not care if the world's foremost deliverance minister came to my town, I would rely solely on the Lord. We may want our pastor to be our deliverance minister, but the Lord may want to use one of the ushers instead. We have to ensure the Lord is leading us especially when we are going through a tribulation; we have to stay close to the Lord. Deliverance is called the children's bread, in part because of what Jesus said to the Canaanite woman who wanted help for her daughter whom demons were tormenting (Matthew 15:22-28). Deliverance is the children's bread, but many of the Lord's children are starving because they are in bondage to the devil. Many people are doing everything they have been told in order to get deliverance. But it is all junk, absolute rubbish, unless the Lord is backing it up. There is no power in any oil unless the anointing of the Lord is in the oil. Like the Lord said, *'And it shall come to pass in that day, that his burden shall be taken away from off thy shoulder, and his yoke from off thy neck, and the yoke shall be destroyed because of the anointing.'* ~ Isaiah 10:27. Many people are questioning the Lord's power because they have not been delivered. Their level of bondage however, provides the perfect set up for the Lord to demonstrate His power because there is no force in the entire universe more powerful than the Lord our God. Jesus is Lord, over all. Jesus is God!

CHAPTER 6

DIVORCED

'Regard not them that have familiar spirits, neither seek after wizards, to be defiled by them: I AM the Lord your God.' ~ Leviticus 19:31

There are two ways in which we can have a familiar spirit. Sure, an evil spirit may reside either inside or outside of the body. But, this relationship dynamic is when the spirit is either a co-laborer or an enemy. In the case of the former, the spirit is forges a covenant as a partnership. But despite its level of service, its job is to secure the human's eternal damnation. The spirit may even let the person believe he or she is in charge, which is a part of its sophisticated masquerade. After such an ill-advised partnership, it will drag the human's soul to hell with it, while gaining access to the children down to the third or fourth generation. If the descendants do not cooperate with the spirit, it will claim to have a legal right to them based on the ancestral or familial covenants. That is until someone demolishes those covenants, once and for all, in the name of Jesus. As you can see from my 11-month battle thus far, it is not always an easy task. The battle depend on several variables, such as:

> **How the initial covenant was forged?** Some ancestors knowingly engaged in witchcraft, possibly for generations. They may have simply consulted with a worker of iniquity, such as a

psychic, witch or sorcerer. Consulting with anyone who partners with a familiar spirit will defile all parties involved. Tragically, some people knowingly sell the souls of their offspring. But rather than selling themselves, or their children, they may seemingly make a deal with the devil where they will not witness the carnage. As a result, they give the devil rights to their grandchildren. The devil does not mind making that deal because he still gets access down to the third and fourth generation, which on his part, is a strategic move. Anyone who sells his or her children, grandchildren, or great grandchildren will have to give an account to the Lord for such wickedness. An even worse scenario is when that ancestor is the worker of iniquity. They often dedicate their children to the kingdom of darkness and train at least one of them as a successor. A person who refuses to partner with a familiar spirit that has been in the family for generations faces a more difficult struggle to get and/or stay free.

Ironically, devils are sticklers for people keeping God's laws, but just so they can pounce on the violators. They will even covertly forge an illegal covenant with righteous people in an effort to gain legal access into their life, such as the "spirit spouses". They know it is illegal, especially because Jesus said marriage is for a man and a woman, and spirits do not marry. They know the "marriage" is illegal, yet will act as if people cannot break the covenant they may have unknowingly formed with the devil, even by willful sin, such as masturbation, fornication and adultery.

How long has the spirit been with a person or the person's family? The spirit is literally like a snake that keeps getting bigger and more powerful with each passing day as it feeds on sin. No wonder Jesus said some spirits only come out through prayer and fasting. It is comparable to starving the spirit to death by not committing sin, which it will try to lead us into to become more powerful. Committing sin also opens the door to reinstate ungodly covenants. Consequently, if we refuse to sin, it will try to either covertly or forcefully reinstate the covenants, even against our will. The spirit is possessive, jealous, and territorial. It sees a person as its property, even someone who has clearly repented and is honoring Christ Jesus. The spirit is jealous of everything good in our life, including the fruit of the Holy Spirit, such as peace and joy. It does not want us to be happy and have peace. Some people will read this and think it perfectly describes their spouse, even though there may not be any demonic entity influencing that spouse.

We should never forget that evil spirits are defiling and everything they do with or to us is meant to defile us with the end result being to steal, kill, and destroy. The saying "Happy wife, happy life" does not apply here. The spirit wants to ensure that we live in misery, and this often involves trying to keep a person single. If that does not work, it will try a "demonically arranged union" by unequally yoking an unbeliever and a Christian. As a result, many people married someone who initially seemed like a gift from God but was a child of satan. The longer the spirit is around, the more challenging it is to unseat it from what it considers its territory. The longer it is in our presence and our family is the more intelligent it becomes on how to attack and counterattack us.

God's will. Jesus cast a legion of demons out of a man in one shot. To this day, I am not quite sure why the Lord allowed the devils to keep coming back into my life, often within hours of being set free. Likewise, it may not be the Lord's will to deliver us from every devil at once. It is easier to live a holy life when we remember our painful struggle, and our hard-fought victory. Jesus told some people to go and sin no more. For some people, if the Lord had made the deliverance process quick and easy, they would have abused His grace and ended up in a worse condition after returning to sin. If that sounds harsh or negative, we should ponder the following:

- "And God saw that the wickedness of man was great in the earth, and that every imagination of the thoughts of his heart was only evil continually." ~ Genesis 6:5
- *'The heart is deceitful above all things, and desperately wicked: who can know it?'* ~ God (Jeremiah 17:9)

My deliverance is a process and I am a work in progress, yet I am more victorious. A major shift occurred on October 17, 2018, after having the following dream:

> ...Several people walked through the house and into a bedroom at the back. The door was partially open and I looked in from a distance. I was surprised when I saw the witch, sitting down by the foot of the bed, like she was mourning, and people were trying to console her. I was pleasantly surprised that I did not get into fight or flight mode. I decided to walk away before she saw me.
>
> I was outside when it sounded like a clan of hyenas fighting over prey. I saw several people trying to restrain the witch on the ground. However, she flicked them off like a warthog using its tusks to repel the hyenas. She kept shouting, "But I hate him! I hate him! I hate him!" I knew she was speaking about me. Then she came over towards me, like we were about to have an old fashion Texas shootout at high noon. She was angry with me for not wanting to marry her, and the subsequent embarrassment it caused. I said the world was going to find out she is a liar, and she charged at me like a bull, but I slipped away and hit her in the process. She passed by and stopped, then came by for another pass. She repeated her charges several times, which meant she got kicked several times. She was like a professional wrestler who was attacking me in the center of the ring by bouncing off the ropes. In wrestling fashion, I even dropkicked her, but she kept coming.
>
> The fight did not last long. One of the things I noticed was she kept getting smaller, until she became a rat on the dark, wet ground, which looked like we were in the middle of a Jamaican street. I stepped on the neck of the rat, severing its head from it body, which caused feces to squirt from its anus.

I woke up and my heart started pounding in my chest as I wondered what just happened. Ironically, today is exactly three years since I saw the witch for the first time. Afterwards, the house felt quiet, as if something spiritual had broken. However, with so many things having transpired, I need the Lord to explain or confirm what just happened. I was inspired to write the following on my two professional Facebook pages:

THE PROCESS: THE REFINER'S FIRE

"Do not let loss be your boss. #ItIsFinished."

"If the Lord said it, He will do it in His unique way and timing."

Despite having that dream, I was not immediately in the clear. There were some demonic manifestations in my house the following day. In addition, I came under intense attack two days after having the dream, which include three dreams where a demon tried seducing me into sexual immorality, a sign that something major was on the horizon. Today is October 24, 2018, the day I made my final edits before sending the manuscript to the editor. Here is a current situation report:

> A friend invited me to a church on Saturday, October 20, 2018 for a function. I went to the church and the pastor invited me to speak to his congregation, which is the first time that has ever happened. I may have spoken for about 20 minutes. Regardless of the time, the pastor let me know the Holy Spirit used me to confirm some things. I did not want to wear out my welcome so I handed the microphone over. Then I was shocked when the guest speaker, did like John the Baptist, and told the entire congregation about my calling from the Lord, I was in tears. It fulfilled what the Lord told me during the deliverance conference. I came all the way out of the cave; mouth first. In addition, the Lord used me to prophesy to a young lady, among other things. In short, everything that happened answered my prayer for vindication after the devil used the pastor at the church the Lord's daughter attended to slander me.
>
> A few days later, on October 23, 2018, the Lord cleared the way for me to give a 45-minute interview on a radio show. I was expecting warfare but things went very smoothly. The Lord also finally gave me the perfect ending to this book, which is a prayer. Then today, I finally finished this manuscript, with 140 pages, just like the Lord had foretold.
>
> Since that time I have been getting more sleep with less demonic activity.

When the Lord says it is our time, no one can stop His plans from coming to fruition. *For the Lord of hosts hath purposed, and who shall disannul it?*

KOLLIN L. TAYLOR

And His hand is stretched out, and who shall turn it back?' ~ Isaiah 14:27

EPILOGUE

'But as for you, ye thought evil against me; but God meant it unto good, to bring to pass, as it is this day, to save much people alive. ~ Joseph (Genesis 50:20)

The devil relentlessly used numerous dirty tricks in an effort to stop me from fulfilling my God-ordained destiny. However, among many things, no one can thwart the Lord's plans. The devil thought Jesus's death was a victory for his kingdom, but now it is Jesus who has the keys to death and hell (Revelation 1:18). Sometimes I envision Jesus having two keys suspended from His waist that makes noise whenever He moves, which serves as a reminder to the devil that he lost and his end is near. The louder the sound of those keys the Lord has is the more it torments the devil to know that he lost the fight. This will not stop him from devising plans to try to delay his public embarrassment to all creation:

> "Wherefore God also hath highly exalted Him, and given Him a name which is above every name and that **at the name of Jesus every knee shall bow**, of things in heaven, and things in earth, and things under the earth; And that **every tongue should confess that Jesus Christ is Lord, to the glory of God the Father**." ~ Philippians 2:9-11

The Lord uses my struggles for His glory. Here are some of the lessons I learned from this absolutely horrible process that I do not wish on my worst enemy, and, I certainly do not want to repeat:

- I do not ever want to enter into a partnership with the devil. I hate having a devil in my presence every day, waiting for me to go to sleep so it can attack me in many despicable ways.
- I do not want to go to hell. This was close enough for me. I do not want anyone to go to hell either, even though many people will get sent there. I knew the Lord was with me throughout the entire process, but it was still very challenging. I am a saved believer, a minister for Christ Jesus, yet suffering at the hands of devils. While I had hope for an end to the afflictions, that is not the case for the numerous professing Christians, including ministers, who are in hell with no hope for redemption. I do not want to feel this far away from the Lord, ever again. Sadly, the only thing worse than feeling distant from the Lord is being eternally separated from Him in hell, the precursor to somewhere worse, the lake of fire.
- I want to break up every ungodly "spiritual marriage". It is better to be single (and celibate) than to have a spirit as a "spouse".
- I hate witchcraft and what it does to people, to include the offspring of those who engage in witchcraft.
- Dogs bark at moving cars. Likewise, when the enemy expends resources to try to stop us, the Lord has great things in store for us, and those we will minister to. When the devil invests resources to fight against us, we should become a greater threat to his kingdom for God's glory.
- I hate satan, almost as much as I hate the spirit that attached itself to me, and, disrespected the name of the Lord Jesus on so many occasions. I literally want to be the one to kick it into the lake of fire for what it did to me and so many other people throughout the ages.
- Whenever the enemy is trying to prevent us from fulfilling our God-ordained destiny, we should engage in spiritual warfare so that he will not come into our life unchallenged. Simultaneously, help others achieve their God-ordained destiny; let the enemy pick his poison. When the Lord blesses us, be a blessing to others. When the devil resists us, especially with a measure of effectiveness, be a blessing to others. This is comparable to a pride of lions that has to focus on taking down one elephant from a herd or they will fail. If we feel like the elephant from the herd with a pride of lion all over

us, remember, "According to their deeds, accordingly He will repay, fury to His adversaries, recompence to His enemies; to the islands He will repay recompence. So shall they fear the name of the Lord from the west, and His glory from the rising of the sun. When the enemy shall come in like a flood, the Spirit of the Lord shall lift up a standard against him." ~ Isaiah 59:18-19

- God is faithful, even when He is testing our faith. It does not matter how things look; trust the Lord. Never forget the power and sovereignty of the Lord, regardless of how much the enemy attacks a promise from the Him to us. *'For the Lord of hosts hath purposed, and who shall disannul it? And His hand is stretched out, and who shall turn it back?'* ~ Isaiah 14:27
- The enemy tries to appear more powerful than the Lord by flooding us with resources, which is similar to junk mail. However, "Ye are of God, little children, and have overcome them: because greater is He that is in you, than he that is in the world." ~ 1 John 4:4. In addition, since the devil only managed to lure a third of the angels away, a choice they will undoubtedly regret in the lake of fire, what Elisha said to his servant also applies to us. *'Fear not: for they that be with us are more than they that be with them.'* ~ 2 Kings 6:16

The Lord said to Israel, *'**My people are destroyed for lack of knowledge:** because thou hast rejected knowledge, I will also reject thee, that thou shalt be no priest to Me: seeing thou hast forgotten the Law of thy God, I will also forget thy children.'* ~ Hosea 4:6. Armed with all this knowledge, let us lock and load a high caliber round to send a fiery dart into the enemy's heart and divorce the devil. Let us pray:

Heavenly Father,

I need You. I rend my heart and not my garments. Father, You are a holy God, the true and living God, there is no God like You, none. Besides You, there is no other God, and even if there were, I choose You. Please forgive me for ALL of my sins, transgressions, and iniquities. Your tender loving mercies are renewed every day, and as you have forgiven me, I forgive every person who has every sinned against me. I release them to You my Lord. Please bless them unto repentance, deliver them from the evil they serve. Please forgive me if anything I held against them was more of an indictment of the condition of my heart instead of their actions, especially if it was something I misunderstood.

Father, You loved this sinful world so You sent Jesus, Your only begotten Son, the perfect and one-time atonement to cleanse the world of its sin. Without the shedding of blood, there is no remission of sin. The perfect shed blood of Jesus cleanses all sins. Father, please wash my scarlet-colored sins until I become as white as snow. The world needs a savior, and that Savior can only be found in Christ Jesus, and Him alone. I commit (*or recommit*) my life to You Jesus and place myself in subjection to You as my Lord and my God. I present my body unto you as a living sacrifice, holy, acceptable unto You my God, as a part of my reasonable service unto You. I thank You for Your forgiveness and for cleansing my sins. Please clothe me in your righteousness.

My righteousness is as filthy rags to You, the Most Holy God. Please baptize me with the Holy Spirit and fire. Heavenly Father, please conform me into the image of Your Son, my Lord and Savior, Jesus the Christ. Let Your Holy Spirit guide me throughout this life that I have now freely and wholeheartedly dedicated unto You. Those who are led by the Spirit of God are the sons of God. You also said I should come out from among them, and touch not the unclean thing, so You will receive me as Your son (*or daughter*). Father, I renounce all other gods and repent of having any other god before you, to include the idols of my heart, such as, marriage, children, career, ministry... Please, create in me a new heart, remove my heart of stone, give me a heart of flesh, and fill me with Your precious Holy Spirit. I renounce the kingdom of darkness, which includes every human and/or impure spirit I have ever partnered with. I repent of those relationships and the resultant covenants. I divorce myself, and my family, from those covenants, and the associated foul spirits, in the name of Jesus. I will not fellowship with the unfruitful works of darkness, but rather, I reprove them in the mighty name of Jesus.

Father, please give me a love for Your Words, and teach me Your ways. Let Your rivers of Living Waters flow from my belly. I humbly ask for Your spirit of wisdom and revelation in the knowledge of You; enlighten the eyes of my understanding that I may know the hope of Your calling. I have tasted and seen that You are good. Please give me opportunities to share Your goodness with others, to include my family, in an effort to lead them unto repentance, and a closer personal relationship with You my Lord. Order my steps my Lord; let Your Word be a lamp unto my feet and a light unto my path. I submit myself to Your lordship and I willing bear the marks of the Lord Jesus. Let Your will be done in my life, here on earth as it is in heaven. I deny myself, pick up my cross, and I willingly follow You Lord Jesus. Thank You my Lord for hearing, but more important, for answering my prayer, in Jesus' name, Amen! I love You.

ABOUT THE AUTHOR

Kollin L. Taylor oversees Social Aloe Ministries where He fulfills his commission from the Lord to "minister to the people." He is a prolific writer and teacher whom the Lord uses to write books and social media posts, and to produce video teachings, to provide edification, exhortation, and comfort to draw people into a deeper personal relationship with Christ Jesus. Based on personal experiences, Kollin is vehemently opposed to spiritual abuse from religious leaders, false prophets, witchcraft and ungodly marriages.

Kollin's published works:

Exposed Part I: The Prelude
Exposed Part II: Romantic Relationships
Exposed Part III: Vida
Exposed Part IV: The Journey Continues
Metamorphosis: The New Me
The Phenom: From My Soul
Resilience: Bend, Don't Break
The Aftermath: When the Smoke Clears and the Dust Settles
Perspective: A New Point of View
The Anatomy of a Heartbreak: When SAMson Met Delilah (narrative)
Round 2: The Battle Continues
Round 3: Still Fighting
Cool Breeze: Irie Man!
Finding Joy in You: The Gift of Eternal Life
Minister to the People: Answering His Calling
The Path to Enlightenment
Knowledge Is Power: Before You Do What You're Told, Know What You're Being Told
Soul Food: Thanks, Lord, for My Daily Bread
Closet Christian: If You Deny Him, He Will Deny You
Australia: A Journey Down Under
Wrongfully Accused: When Innocence Is Not Enough

KOLLIN L. TAYLOR

The Sidelines: Those Who Can ...
Flirting with Disaster
The Sound of a Fallen Tree
Survival
Humble Pie: A Gift from God
Second Chances: Worthy of Redemption
God's Kitchen: His Slow Cooked Stew
On Trial: A Test of My Faith
God Speaks to My Soul
God, the Love of My Life
Labor Pains: Waiting to Push!
Breakthrough: When Jesus Sets You Free
Born Again: Renew Your Mind with the Holy Spirit
Holy Spirit Led: My Steps Are Ordered
Raised in the Wilderness: Rogue Reformers, Rallying the Remnant
So, You Want to be a Prophet... ARE YOU CRAZY?

The Process: The Refiner's Fire is Kollin's 39th book.

Author photo by **Kendall Herman Photography**

Made in the USA
Monee, IL
27 August 2020